S. J. Perelman

Twayne's United States Authors Series

Warren French, Editor

Indiana University, Indianapolis

TUSAS 436

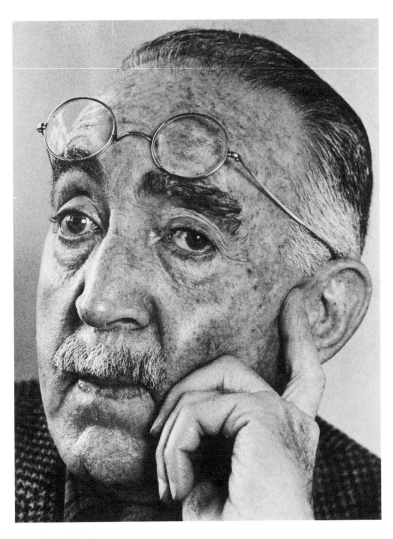

S. J. PERELMAN
(1904–1979)
Photograph courtesy of The Tallahassee Democrat

S.J. Perelman

By Douglas Fowler
Florida State University

Twayne Publishers · Boston

S. J. Perelman

Douglas Fowler

Copyright © 1983 by G. K. Hall & Company
All Rights Reserved
Published by Twayne Publishers
A Division of G. K. Hall & Company
70 Lincoln Street
Boston, Massachusetts 02111

Book Production by Marne B. Sultz
Book Design by Barbara Anderson

Printed on permanent/durable acid-free
paper and bound in the United States of
America.

Library of Congress Cataloging in Publication Data

Fowler, Douglas.
  S. J. Perelman.

  (Twayne's United States authors series ;
  TUSAS 436)
  Bibliography: p. 159
  Includes index.
  1. Perelman, S. J. (Sidney Joseph), 1904—1979.
2. Authors, American—20th century—Biography.
I. Title.   II.   Series.
PS3531.E6544Z65   1983   818'5209 [B]   82-18723
ISBN 0-8057-7376-2

For David Kirby,
living well is the best revenge

Contents

About the Author

Douglas Fowler grew up in Columbia, Missouri, and received a B.A., M.F.A., and Ph.D. from Cornell University, where he won literary competitions in fiction, playwriting, and poetry. He served in the U.S. Army in Oklahoma and Germany, and is currently professor of English at Florida State University. *Reading Nabokov* was published by Cornell University Press in 1974, and *A Reader's Guide to Gravity's Rainbow* by Ardis in 1980. His writings have appeared in the *Yeats-Eliot Review*, the *South Atlantic Quarterly*, *Studies in Popular Culture*, and the *Journal of Popular Culture*. He is presently at work on a study of the spy fiction of John le Carré.

Preface

From the early 1930s until his death in 1979, one of the most interesting and accomplished of American comic voices was that of S. J. Perelman, and of all the writers who have attempted to create an American comic perspective in those years Perelman's efforts may have been the most distinctive and the most likely to weather the future. This is a large claim to make about a writer who has deliberately imposed upon his work severe limitations as to its focus, intentions, and technique, and I would immediately agree that it would be a mistake to claim for Perelman "major" status: he never undertook the novel form or the serious discursive essay; his pieces never show personality in a process of growth or change; his intention was solely to amuse and delight for almost fifty professional years. He worked in balsawood, not marble, and we cannot find in his work any direct attention to our most urgent human concerns—life, death, sexuality, loss, choice, freedom, power, moral dilemma; we cannot expect it to show us ourselves. Perelman was a toymaker; a professional toymaker, perhaps one of the most gifted who ever lived by that craft. But it would be a misleading mistake to confuse his craft with portraiture, architecture, or the manufacture of weapons—with that of the novelist, the theorist, or the satirist. Literary people are too quick to try to attach serious moral purposes to Perelman and to assume that because we know he was a man who found the world a dangerous and disappointing place (and he told us again and again that he did), his comic writing must in some way embody that truth. Must it? The rhetorical shape of that question has already alerted you to the fact that I believe otherwise and hope to show why. In a study he calls *The American Humorist: Conscience of the Twentieth Century*, Norris W. Yates claims that behind Perelman's facade of cartoon and parody "lurk the same values" that a Stoic philosopher or a Scoutmaster would applaud: "integrity, sincerity, skepticism, taste, a respect for competence, a striving after the golden mean, and a longing for better communication and understanding among men." We might well come to agree that Perelman the man was the very embodiment of every virtue listed, but in coming to appreciate him as an artist we may find such a catalog confusing and inadequate. An artistic truth can be complex and full of contradictions, and it might not be entirely flattering to the artist and his audience, either.

Perelman was a master technician with prose and a remarkably skillful comic strategist, and he did the small things he chose to do with wonderful precision. But like most creation which celebrates its own form over its own content, Perelman's work has become famous as a style and yet largely ignored as a mode of sensibility. The most neglected but intriguing artists are sometimes not the avant-garde or the esoteric, but the overfamiliar: artists who have disqualified themselves from serious (or pseudo-serious) attention through their own lack of fashionability. We can draw a parallel from the visual arts. The proper noun "Norman Rockwell" suggests the sort of gauche, empty, middle-American sentimentality that no serious critic can afford to admire, and no person of cultivation could hang a Rockwell in his home except by way of a joke. But in point of fact a vintage *Saturday Evening Post* cover by Rockwell can be appreciated not only for its technical excellence (which has never been in dispute) but also for its fine portrayal of those very sentimental emotions it sought to express in the first place—for it is always the cardinal mistake of the humanities establishment to suppose that because an emotion is large and common and primary-colored and the possession of the unglamorous that it does not really exist. As Gerard Manley Hopkins once said, common sense is never out of place anywhere.

Perelman was always playful and he always worked in small forms, and so, although his name has become a label, a descriptive adjective, the distinctiveness of his achievement has never been closely defined. He continued a tradition; he had influence; a tradition continues from him. When the British-born critic Martin Green came to read Salinger and Nabokov, he discovered in both "a style characterised by its exuberant and recondite vocabulary, highly literary and highly technical at the same time, lavish of foreign phrases, commercial terms, academic turns of speech . . . its images . . . extremely clever, its manner consistently self-concious, its effects all variations on a theme of exaggeration," and that the America described in *Lolita* and

Franny is "most unlike the broad shafts of sunlight bathing the broad and noble cornfields in ordinary poetic descriptions of America." What Green recognized in that urbane and self-conscious artificiality is Perelman's influence and Perelman's sensibility, for I hope to persuade the reader that one of the most uniquely American of writers turns out to be everything we have supposed an American writer is not: Jewish, playful, urban, artificial, an exquisite stylist, erudite, shrill, small, and negative. For a culture that has been calling *Moby-Dick* its greatest epic and Hemingway its archetypal artist-hero for the last fifty years, the idea of Perelman as a lens for looking into an important aspect of national sensibility may seem almost indecent: and yet it is true, just as it is true that Gogol's voice contains and explains as much of Russia as Tolstoy's, or that Lewis Carroll's voice is as real to the English experience as Hardy's, or that Ambrose Bierce's eerie and morbid gothicism is as central to the American experience as William Dean Howells's yea-saying. It is the purpose of this book to suggest how.

The first three chapters of this book follow Perelman's career more or less chronologically. Chapter 1 tells of his schooling, his friendship with Nathanael West at Brown University, his years in Greenwich Village, his connections with the Marx Brothers, and his other efforts in the Hollywood celluloid mills. Chapter 2 centers on Perelman's work for Mike Todd's *Around the World in Eighty Days* and takes a look at his Broadway plays *One Touch of Venus* and *The Beauty Part*. Chapter 3 recounts Perelman's adventures in the television trade and offers some speculation about the manner in which his approach altered and darkened a bit over the course of his career, using his accounts of a meeting with Ernest Hemingway as illustration. Chapter 4 is an attempt to place Perelman inside both American and Jewish comedy sensibilities. Chapter 5 discusses Perelman's comic techniques in terms of his travel, the household, and nostalgia as points of departure, and Chapter 6 discusses his influence among other writers and hazards a guess as to how the future may come to regard his achievement.

Douglas Fowler

Florida State University

Chronology

1936   Writes *Florida Special* with Laura for Paramount.

1937   *Strictly From Hunger*, Perelman's first collection of *New Yorker* pieces.

1939   With Laura, co-scripts *Ambush* for Paramount. Hosts a summer radio quiz show on whodunit theme, *Author, Author!*

1940   *Look Who's Talking*. Collaborates on screenplay for MGM's *The Golden Fleecing*.

1941   Play coauthored with Laura, *The Night Before Christmas*, at New York's Morosco Theater.

1943   With Ogden Nash, writes the book for the musical comedy *One Touch of Venus*, with Mary Martin in the title role.

1944   *Crazy Like a Fox* and *One Touch of Venus*.

1946   *Sweet Bye and Bye*, a musical with a futuristic theme, closes in Philadelphia during tryouts. *Keep It Crisp*.

1947   *Acres and Pains* and *The Best of S. J. Perelman*.

1948   *Westward Ha!*

1949   Voyages to the South Seas, Micronesia, and the Orient with family.

1950   *The Swiss Family Perelman*.

1952   *The Ill-Tempered Clavicord*.

1953   Trip to East Africa.

1955   *Perelman's Home Companion*. Begins work for Mike Todd on script for *Around the World in Eighty Days*.

1956   Co-winner of both Academy Award and New York Film Critics Award for screenwriting Todd's epic.

1957   Staff writer for NBC's *Omnibus* series.

1958   Writes script for Cole Porter television musical, *Aladdin*. *The Most of S. J. Perelman*.

1959   *Malice in Wonderland*, a satiric spoof on Hollywood, telecast on *Omnibus*.

1961 *The Rising Gorge.*

1962 *The Beauty Part*, with Bert Lahr, in midst of 114-day New York City newspaper strike.

1963 *The Beauty Part* closes. Writes *Elizabeth Taylor's London*, a CBS special.

1966 *Chicken Inspector No. 23.*

1970 Laura West Perelman dies April 10. Perelman sells his Bucks County farm and moves to London in October. *Baby, It's Cold Inside.*

1971 Trip around the world retracing Phileas Fogg's journey.

1972 Returns to New York City.

1974 Revival of *The Beauty Part* at American Place Theater.

1975 *Vinegar Puss* reviewed by Eudora Welty on first page of *New York Times.*

1977 *Eastward Ha!*

1978 Receives first Special Achievement Award of the National Book Awards Committee.

1979 "Portrait of the Artist as a Young Cat's-Paw," his last comic essay in *New Yorker*. Dies of cardiac arrest in his apartment at the Grammercy Park Hotel, October 17.

Chapter One
Heroes and Bookworms

Perelman's Appeal

Sidney Joseph Perelman was born in Brooklyn in 1904 and grew up in Providence, Rhode Island. His father, after failed careers as a marine engineer, machinist, and dry goods dealer, finally settled down to raising poultry. The family was always poor. "Whatever he did, there wasn't much money,"[1] Perelman said of his father's efforts to put a life together for his family here in the New World. And yet if there was little money, there were always books. "You'd go to the library with a bookstrap Friday afternoon and bring your load of books back, all read, Monday morning,"[2] Perelman told *Life* for an article about him significantly titled "The Cranky Humorist." And yet according to our national mythology, American boys are not supposed to be cranky bookworms, and American boys who become famous professional writers should at least arrange to have outdoor boyhoods in the tradition of Twain, Faulkner, Hemingway, and Steinbeck. But Perelman's boyhood—at least that portion of it he allows us to glimpse in his writing—was largely a matter of vicarious adventure and borrowed romance, with danger and heroism at one remove. The magic carpet always went back to the library on Monday morning. "When the Princess Pats stood at Passchendaele in '17, I was damned careful to be twelve years old and three thousand miles to the rear, selling Domes of Silence after school to the housewives of Crescent Park, Rhode Island" (*M*, 433),[3] Perelman begins one of his pieces. In another he tells of how, "against overwhelming odds I collected peach pits and tin foil for gas masks in 1918."[4]

More than half of Perelman's approximately 400 published pieces were generated out of his response to an item he had read, be it an authentic masterpiece like *Ulysses* or a wisp of advertising ephemera he has come across in a mail-order catalog. In fact, of all the writers in our national heritage, one might reasonably claim that Perelman is perhaps the most bookish. Paradoxically, this pen-and-ink insubstantiality is one source of his enduring appeal, and one must look again at the unoffical realities of American literary culture to see why this might be so. Several large generalizations are unavoidable.

Civilizations always begin outdoors and in the masculine gender, and the civilization of the United States is obviously no exception. If all our lives we have heard those clichés about the white man's ax ringing in the virgin wilderness while the Conestoga wagons and the Iron Horse crept inch by inevitable inch out toward the Pacific and our manifest destiny, we ought to remember that clichés are only clichés because they are true—or at least true enough. America was a frontier civilization until well into this century (Arizona was admitted to statehood as recently as 1912). The Spanish-American War, World War I, the Roaring Twenties, the depression, World War II, Korea, the Cold War, Vietnam—for the last seventy-five years our national experience seems to have been exclusively picturesque, martial, rowdy, melodramatic, and exterior. And as for those heroic or pseudo-heroic figures who come to seem archetypical of a nation's identity, one need only mention Teddy Roosevelt, Henry Ford, Babe Ruth, Will Rogers, Charles Lindbergh, John Wayne, Walt Disney, Jack Kennedy, Ronald Reagan, or even Martin Luther King to indicate how pronounced is that streak of active, impatient, extroverted boyishness in our national psyche. Our history seems to be the history of boy-men doing things. Of course this boyishness is contrived, and we can take as axiomatic a good deal of pretense in regard to its cultivation. It is obviously not the whole story. But as far as any such simplification can be made to stand up, those names tell us a good deal about the way our civilization has wanted to think of itself. There simply has not yet been a female, artistic or intellectual figure with whom we could feel comfortable here in America. Eleanor Roosevelt was perceived as an admirable but comic anomaly, a fate that also overtook Mae West. I have already made reference to Norman Rockwell as a gifted sentimentalist, and it is important to remember that he is beyond all comparison the most beloved graphic artist in our heritage. But it would be difficult to imagine a more public, exterior sort of image or an art with less inner life and mystery than one of Rockwell's vintage *Saturday Evening Post* covers. Our most famous intellectual, Albert Einstein, was a European-Jewish émigré whose celebrity depended less on his origination of theories proving that what your common sense told you was true really wasn't than it did on his persona as the caricature of shaggy absent-minded genius with chalk-dust on its sleeve.

The degree to which we Americans have always committed ourselves to a self-image of active and unlettered boyishness becomes clear by way of contrast if we think of definitive Britishers like Charles Darwin, Gilbert and Sullivan, Oscar Wilde, Bertrand Russell, G. B. Shaw, Dylan Thomas, the duke of Windsor, or T. S. Eliot, whose transformation from St. Louis high bourgeois to royalist, Anglican, classicist, and British subject in 1927 seems a perfect paradigm to illustrate the cultural gulf I am speaking of here. Until very recently, then, America was taught to think of itself in Scoutmaster terms, and the official national myth was a Scoutmaster myth. The reality, like all realities, was different, and literary people were perhaps the first to discover that fact. Real life, they found out, was not going to be as much fun as *Tarzan of the Apes* or *Black Beauty* read under the covers by flashlight, or that it was going to be only via books and films that they could enter for a privileged moment a world more interesting than this one ever seemed to be. They did not take part in thrilling adventures; they went to graduate school.

Comedy originates in disappointment; it is a means of revenging oneself on the interval between the imagined and the actual, and S. J. Perelman is a great comic writer for all of us literary, unadventurous people because his response to this disappointment, his revenge on reality, is simply a more gifted version of ours. Like so many of us, he never had real adventures to compare with the ones he read about; and so for us, he has transmuted this disappointment into comic gold. "I am insouciant—and very sad,"[5] Perelman once said, pointing out that one of the basic motives animating his comedy was "the constant repetition of one's helplessness in a majority of situations."[6] Comic writing was to him a release from anger, a balm for disappointment-bruises: "I'm highly irritable and my senses bruise easily, and when they are bruised I write."[7] Eudora Welty, speaking of Perelman's 1970 collection *Baby, It's Cold Inside*, points out that in "back of these pieces, and not very far, lies deep sadness, lies outrage."[8] And so for those people to whom books are more than important, Perelman's style of comedy has been irresistible for more than forty years. Its surface is bookishly erudite, and literary people have been flattered to discover a thousand references to their own world reflected on this shimmering quicksilver. Perelman's audience recognizes and congratulates itself for recognizing an allusion to *Finnegans Wake* in a title like "Anna Trivia Pluralized," or a casual tribute to *Moby-Dick* in his ending a piece on the failure of a play with the mock-elegiac phrase, "I alone, Ishmael, was left clinging to a spar."[9]

Among contemporary writers perhaps only Vladimir Nabokov is as bookishly allusive as Perelman, and literary people have been delighted to find both writers putting their specialized world and its particulars put to such elegant use. Perelman speaks directly to the English literature major when he casually alludes to Charles Dickens's boyhood apprenticeship in a blacking factory, or characterizes the genepool of a decayed Florida hamlet as being "obviously subsidized by Carson McCullers to furnish her with literary material,"[10] or describes his own appearance in an overlarge rented tuxedo with an image from Shelley: "Two vast and trunkless legs, like those of Ozymandias."[11] Nor is Perelman's allusiveness reserved only for graduate-school fare. He is in fact America's most distinguished curator of those works of art and near-art that we have come to call Great Bad Books. The Sherlock Holmes stories, *The Mystery of Dr. Fu Manchu*, *Trail of the Lonesome Pine*, *Kidnapped*, *Graustark*, *Girl of the Limberlost*, *Scaramouche*—Perelman calls up memories of our first experience with thriller literature with vividness and affection, presenting himself in a sort of verbal snapshot of imaginative levitation that we can all recognize: wet-socked feet drying in the oven (this is, after all, Rhode Island), "eyes protruding a half inch from their sockets, wolfing ginger snaps,"[12] Perelman at twelve or thirteen is an Everyman for those of us who grew up to be bookworms, too, a class that in America has probably numbered in the tens of thousands for at least three generations—perhaps the largest and most important of the unacknowledged classes in an officially classless society for the simple reason that bookish people do America's college teaching, write its novels, record its history, define its manners and attitudes, even help shape its opinions. But if the pen is mightier than the sword, it has also been held a good deal less glamorous. And here Perelman is our inkpot Siegfried, a reader's-and-writer's writer whose tastes are ours and whose talents are essentially magnified versions of our own.

Ernest Hemingway's once-immense reputation could serve a convenient measure for the scorn with which mere literary playfulness and words for their own sake were "officially" regarded at the beginning of the Vietnam era. Papa always suspected words would only defile the purity of experience (which is to say, the experience of human or animal death, Hemingway's only real interest). Words should not be seen, but seen through, and for about forty years Hemingway's views and technique dominated American letters. The minimalist vocabulary; the tiresome melodrama of war, hunting and fishing; the shallow, inexpressive, monosyllabic rhetoric which everyone agreed to call biblical—as long as writing was held to be only a windowpane onto events and not an event in itself—made writers like Perelman, Nabokov, Bellow, and Salinger seem minor, parochial, or arty in comparison with the author of *The Old Man and the Sea*.

But no civilization stays oudoors and boyish forever, and the maturing transformation wrought in our national psyche by the Vietnam debacle, by the civil rights struggle, and by the impact of feminism all seem to have left us with a mandate to reassess the achievements of the literary imagination in our time. This reassessment can only enhance Perelman's reputation, and enhancement is long overdue.

Writing in 1968, John Hollander pointed out that Perelman's influence on contemporary writers has been consistently either ignored or slighted: "Perelman in particular remains one of the under-acknowledged masters and teachers; among other things, he seems to have made the comic regions of *Ulysses* accessible to a whole generation which has begun to come to terms with the undeniable sanctity and sublimity of low comedy."[13] Perelman is then at once familiar and forgotten, and it is somehow necessary to keep insisting that he has been a significant factor in American writing for at least two generations of literary artists.

Writer's Boyhood—and Beyond

Sooner or later every writer is asked why he writes, a query that Perelman once responded to by quoting from George Orwell's famous essay "Why I Write." Orwell gives four motives for all writing: aesthetic enthusiasm, the effort to set down history as it really happened, the use of words as political implements are three of them. But Perelman claimed the first of Orwell's motives was by far the most significant in his own writing career: "Orwell called this 'sheer egotism,' and he cited the desire to get your own back on insults and rebuffs suffered in childhood. And that is my reason exactly."[14]

Specific instances for those insults and rebuffs remain a matter of conjecture, for Perelman was always reticent about his childhood, boyhood, and young manhood as "a fur-bearing adolescent" growing up absurd on the "rim of Narragansett Bay"(M, 453). Despite spectacular differences in their attitudes toward it, both Sam Levenson and Philip Roth have helped to make the standard male-Jewish childhood into something of an American folk-motif, but Perelman neither sentimentalized nor psychiatrized his identity as a Jew. Although his parents had arrived in America from Russia only a few years before Sidney was born, Joseph and Sophia Perelman did not send their son to Hebrew school or enforce on him an especially pronounced religious or ethnic self-consciousness. The elder Perelman had been a marine engineer aboard the *Morro Castle* in Havana Harbor in 1898 when the U. S. S. *Maine* was blown up by the Spanish and the United States entered upon its shortest and most popular war, featuring the famous Rough Rider heroics on San Juan Hill that freed Cuba from European domination. The sight of sharks feeding on the bodies of American sailors from the *Maine* was no doubt one experience that sent Joseph Perelman back to Rhode Island and that series of unsuccessful occupations on dry (but at least sharkless) land.

Little Sidney was not discouraged from being artistic as a boy, and he remembers drawing cartoons "on the long cardboard strips around which the bolts of Amoskeag cotton and Ginghams were stored"[15] in his father's dry-goods shop (the loving accuracy of the adjective "Amoskeag" is a characteristic Perelman touch, incidentally: part of his responsibility as curator of the precious and fragile past).

Along with his business failures, Joseph Perelman lost money on an ill-starred venture to make Sir Walter Scott's *The Heart of Midlothian* into a Yiddish musical. But we might be safe in assuming that a father interested enough in the arts to lose money backing them is a pretty good father for a creative son to have. And yet other than the barest facts and some very guarded vignettes, Perelman never shows us much of his early years, and it is characteristic that the incidents he has chosen to reveal are almost all recollections of what he was reading or watching at the time.

For example, in 1914 when Perelman was ten, a sixth grader at Candace Street Grammar School and "too wispy" to stand up to the class bully, he did manage to create for himself a future as a hybrid of African explorer and private detective, and the most significant event of his school year was the discovery of Theda Bara as "The Vampire" in *A Fool There Was*. 1916 is secured for us less through Perelman's recollections of his private life than for the fact that it was then he read *The Mystery of Dr. Fu Manchu*, Sax Rohmer's overheated racist epic about the threat to the West from the Yellow Peril and its most hideous incarnation, the evil genius from China whose "long, magnetic eyes of true cat green" are veiled by a reptilian nictating membrane and who concentrates within his own person "all the cruel cunning of an entire Eastern race" (*M*, 454).

1916 was also the first time that Perelman saw the Marx brothers, then doing a vaudeville act called *Home Again* that included lines from Groucho like "the next time I cross the ocean, I'll take a train" (*M*, 625) but at least set in motion the machinery of fate that was eventually to bring Perelman out to Hollywood to help create *Monkey Business* and *Horse Feathers*.

Foreshadowing his destiny as a writer, Perelman won first prize in a nation-wide essay contest sponsored by the *American Boy* in 1917. His entry was entitled "Grit" and extolled that virtue in the famous Parisian taxi drivers who helped transport French infantrymen to the banks of the Marne to stem the German advance.

Perelman almost always turns to his imaginative life to mark out a major event for each year of his adolescence: thus, 1918 was the year he discovered *Tarzan of the Apes*, Edgar Rice Burroughs's great boy's classic, and in 1919, when he was fifteen, he tells us that his spells of puppy-love were directed less toward the palpable girls of Providence than the phantasms created by Elinor Glyn in her famous and fatuous romance, *Three Weeks*. As for the movies, Perelman found Gloria Swanson in Cecil B. DeMille's *Male and Female* a good deal more compelling than the Gallic commentaries of Caesar he was translating at Classical High School. So although he might be discovered shifting ashes out of the neighborhood's coal-stoked furnaces or beating the dust out of (nonflying) carpets for thirty-five cents an hour, Perelman's real life was being lived by means of the printed page, the subtitled screen, and the vaudeville stage. By his senior year in high school, 1921, Perelman had not only left behind him a legion of "dead and dying gerunds" writhing on Xenophon's stony Mesopotamian plain, he had also committed his first peculation in the cause of art: as editor of the student literary magazine, the *Accolade*, he borrowed its circulation advances in order to finance a day's hookey in the fleshpots of Boston, and at a Shubert vaudeville house there he first witnessed the "saucy tomfoolery" of Fred Allen (then billing himself as "the World's Worst Juggler"). Perelman's illicit excursion might have been better concealed if he had been able to forego three pounds of salt-water taffy mixed with Durgin Park's corn bread, clam chowder, and strawberry shortcake, but a gargantuan stomachache inevitably led to his discovery: "I still carry a welt on my crupper engraved there by my father's belt buckle." Small enough price to pay for an afternoon appreciating the World's Worst Juggler.

High School and College

Like many a young man from a poor family, Perelman held down some boring, dangerous, and bizarre jobs, and was poorly paid for doing them. For a time he electroplated automobile radiators at one of the flimsy little factories that mushroomed all over the American landscape before production became centralized in Detroit. Noxious fumes from the acid baths into which it was Perelman's duty to plunge honeycomb radiators stripped him of eleven pounds he could ill afford to lose and gave him persistent nightmares, and his parents, notwithstanding their own financial straits, finally persuaded him to quit. Since he would "sooner have parted with a lung than missed such epochal attractions as *Tol'able David* or Rudolph Valentino in *The Four Horsemen of the Apocalypse,*" Perelman worked in a department store bakery (from which he was fired for swiping some whipped marshmallow out of a tureen), sold vacuum cleaners door-to-door ("I was met everywhere by vast apathy"), caddied at a golf course, and night-clerked in a cigar store. Anything for art and the thirty-five cents admission fee it cost to view it.

In school, the Classical High debating team occupied that portion of Perelman's attention left over after the legitimate deductions he made in it for movies, radiators, and girls. "Resolved: That the Philippines Should Be Given Their Independence." "Resolved: That The Pen Is Mightier Than The Sword." Taking the part of science versus religion, Perelman as chairman cautioned the Vatican "under pain of my displeasure" to allow science to flourish in the sunshine of sweet and unsuperstitious reason. The Vatican's response is not on record.

In 1921 Perelman graduated from high school and, with a good deal of strain on his father's precarious finances, enrolled in Brown University. Fifty years later Alan Brien was startled to find Perelman finally admitting to some real resentment at the anti-Semitism that was then endemic on Ivy League campuses: "There were nineteen fraternities. As a Jew, I wasn't invited to join any of them. That is, until I started to write and became editor of the humor magazine. Then two of them asked me to belong. I refused them flat, and that gave me great pleasure." For a time Perelman followed a premedical curriculum, but obviously a regimen centering on the dissection of "the nervous system of simple invertebrates (including our parents')" was not going to captivate a comic genius with printer's ink in his veins. The campus humor magazine was the *Brown Jug*, but Perelman also drew cartoons for the literary magazine, *Casements*—it was still years before he would sell his soul to the muse of print. At the beginning of a piece detailing a revisit to his sophomore days, Perelman recalls how he illustrated with pagan scenes cribbed from Aubrey Beardsley the pagan verse his classmates cribbed from a wonderfully silly novel called *Wife of the Centaur*. But *Casements* soon collapsed from complications of acute plagiarization, and Perelman marched on toward his destiny as a comic writer.

The destiny of another writer soon intertwined with his own.

Nathanael von Wallenstein Weinstein transferred to Brown from Tufts in 1922, where he legally changed his name to Nathanael West. The man who was to win enduring literary fame as the creator of *Miss Lonelyhearts* and *The Day of the Locust* immediately attracted Perelman. People who loved the arts were beginning to cluster together; it was a sign of the times. In reaction to the noisy, red-baiting, patriotic cant and muscular repressiveness of Prohibition, many artistic and literary Americans in the 1920s opted for expatriation and even exile, some of it literal. Hemingway and Fitzgerald were of course the most famous of them, but Gertrude Stein of Oakland, California, spoke for many sensitive and talented people when she characterized her birthplace with one of those Delphic aphorisms that now constitute her only enduring legacy: "There's no there there." A good many of the best and the brightest were finding no there there in postwar America, and even if they could not emulate Stein and actually relocate in Paris— "Paris was where the Twentieth Century was," as she said—they adopted a superior and scornful attitude toward their own society that was only partially a pose.

Perelman and West were drawn together because they were not enthusiasts for a boyish, bullish, outdoorsy America indiscriminately in love with itself. Calvin Coolidge and his dictum "The business of America is business," the Eighteenth Amendment, the resurgence of the KKK, Henry Ford, Mary Pickford's cloying screen persona (a curious amalgam of saccharine and stainless steel), and the Scopes "Monkey Trial" in Tennessee might be useful codes with which to particularize our official national persona, and the young and intelligent frequently found themselves at odds with the times. On college campuses an "aesthetic" point of view became an acceptable minority fashion.

Perelman and West shared an enthusiasm for James Joyce and dadaists, and Perelman wrote an editorial for *Casements* that was a sort of affectionate parody of West as an acolyte of Oscar Wilde: It was called "The Exquisites: A Divigation," and plaintively asked of America "where can we find the Paters and Beardsleys of this generation?"[16] The literary fashion was to emulate *fin de siècle* modes like the *Yellow Book*, and Perelman and West helped form a very loose-knit group of litterateurs who called themselves "the Hanseatic League."

Perelman has described his set as being made up of those thorny apostles of art and culture and antiphilistinism who "belonged to Mencken." His editorials were of course imitations of Mencken's jeremiads in the *American Mercury*, and Perelman has since acknowledged that he learned a good deal by borrowing a sensibility from the sage of Baltimore: "H. L. Mencken was the Catherine wheel, the ultimate firework. . . . With his use of the colloquial and the dynamic, the foreign reference, and the bizarre word like *Sitzfleisch* he brought adrenaline into the gray and pulpy style of the day."[17]

Perelman and West

As undergraduates neither Perelman nor West could be accused of gray pulpiness. West, a year ahead of Perelman, was in appearance an affected dandy; Perelman insists it was merely the protective coloration of a sensitive dreamer: "when I got to know him he had a warm and fanciful humor and great erudition that made the rest of us feel sort of juvenile."[18] The admiration was reciprocated, and then some. Even after he became a much-discussed novelist, West gave Lillian Hellman the impression that his friendship with Perelman had been crucial in his imaginative development,[19] and West was always to insist that Perelman was a great writer whose work would live. During their college friendship, Perelman designed an ex-libris bookplate for West that celebrated their shared disdain for the crowd even while pretending to mock their own feelings of superiority. The caption of the bookplate was a quote from Goethe: "Do I love what others love?" The drawing with which Perelman accompanied it depicted a man with his arm around the neck of a jackass. Perelman had difficulty getting West to pay him for the bookplate, but not because of the sentiment it expressed.

Although they scorned Percy Marks's ephemeral bestselling novel, *The Plastic Age*, Perelman and West must surely have coveted for themselves the reality of fame when they saw the young instructor-novelist affecting a walking-stick under Brown's academic elms; Perelman saw that Marks was at least not one of the "doddering old professors."[20] Surely great artistic things lay before them, if one simply had the perseverance. Art was everything. And one has only to

look again at an astonishing statement made by Mencken's colleague
on the *Smart Set* and then the *American Mercury*, George Jean Nathan,
to sense the strength of that devotion. As Nathan put it in "The Code
of a Critic": "The great problems of the world—social, political,
economic, and theological—do not concern me in the slightest. . . .
If all the Armenians were to be killed tomorrow, [the Turks] and half
the Russians were to starve to death the day after, it would not matter
to me in the least . . . my sole interest is in writing."[21] A cynical,
snobbish claim like that would be fiercely attacked in our era, of
course; no doubt it was in some measure a pose. But the mere fact that
an influential critic and a major intellectual journal could assume such
a Wildean art-for-art's-sake pose offers us some insight into the
origins of Perelman's career. The objects of Perelman's comic attack
have always been style, not substance, and we have only to contrast his
work with, say, Philip Roth's *Our Gang* (a savage satire on Richard
Nixon), Joseph Heller's *Catch-22* (a savage satire on the absurdity of
war), or Kurt Vonnegut's "Harrison Bergeron" (a savage and tiresome
satire on enforced equality) to see the difference in mental atmosphere. Beneath its technical devices, American comic writing now
tends toward the school of Jonathan Swift—or at least the school of
Ralph Nader. "Satire is a lesson, parody is a game," as Vladimir
Nabokov put it. But Perelman has always been far more interested in
the game than in the lesson.

The "Real World"

The years immediately following college are an ordeal for most
American writers and artists. Having occupied themselves with the
great achievements of Western culture for what are really the crown-
ing years of their adolescence, they are at once as ambitious as Faust
and as frightened as a country mouse, overwhelmed by a desperate
need to be not just competent or promising or professional, but great.
Nothing less than greatness will do. The idea of apprenticeship, a
gradual and systematic development of skills by imitation, does not
fit the American psyche very well. The premise of rugged individual-
ism, of creating oneself instantaneously from next to nothing, is
peculiarly American, and it unconsciously affects our artists, too. But

in the arts it is almost impossible to create oneself *ad hoc* and right now, for one does not simply stumble on genius (even if one possesses genius). Just like the rest of us, the genius must find his own limits, his own métier.

The Waste Land appeared like a dark miracle in 1922, and its glamor for young American writers was impossible to overestimate. Joyce's *Ulysses* was completed the same year and was soon in mildly illegal circulation among English-speaking literati—and even its alleged "obscenity" (Judge Woolsey's famous decision allowing it to be published in the United States would have to wait until 1933) gave it a fashionable cachet and further intensified the feeling that the artist was a rebel against the pulpy-gray repressiveness of philistine morality. If you were going to devote yourself to the arts, you were *ipso facto* a bohemian. And after Paris—a long way after—the only place for the artist-bohemian to breathe was in Greenwich Village, New York City. Perelman relocated there in 1925.

His ordeal was real enough, perhaps milder than most. He was going to be a great cartoonist. Both *Judge* and *College Humor* had published a few of Perelman's drawings while he was still an undergraduate, and *Judge* retained him at very modest salary to furnish their pages with some cartoons. But the magazine "rejected everything I drew"[22] even though it published some of his prose. Perelman describes one of his ill-starred cartoons as depicting a man desperately hauling a friend into a doctor's office and whimpering, "I've got Bright's disease and he has mine." If no one laughed, or bought, he had still convinced himself "by incredible sophistry" that fame was just around the corner. It was, but that corner would be turned with words, not pictures. And before he got there, Perelman would have to undergo some excruciating bohemian moments.

During their senior year at Brown Perelman and a colleague on the *Brown Jug* he calls "Conrad Portnoy" had made a trip to Manhattan, where they had stayed gratis in hotels that had exchanged free passes for advertising in the college magazine. Even if that visit had been less than successful—"No bellboy could direct us to a midnight orgy"[23]— the July after graduation Perelman and Portnoy moved to Baghdad-on-the-subway together. For a time they lived in a rooming house on West Twelfth Street, but their mascara-daubed and bangled belle of a landlady ("The clash of bracelets as she moved sounded like Mosby's cavalry unsheathing their sabres for a charge")[24] soon married a chiropodist who needed Perelman's room for an office. In any event, the young cartoonist had been having difficulties making funny drawings under the eyes of a stuffed baby giraffe whose counterweighted head shook in disapproval at the slightest vibration.

Portnoy simply could not make a go of anything in New York and departed for Cleveland and an insurance firm; the next couple of years at least left Perelman free to satisfy to the limit his taste for bohemian decor. More or less on the rebound from living in a series of tacky Village rooms with roommates to match, Perelman converted a skylighted walkup near Jefferson Market Court into a seductive den of monk's cloth, incense, and candle-wax. The girls he brought up to see his etchings never seemed to succumb to the erotic atmosphere, and when Perelman subleased the place to a pair of "decorous young chaps of good family"[25] while he took himself to Fire Island for a six-weeks vacation, his "bedding, utensils, curtains and Capehart" vanished into the middle distance. Since Perelman had spent his Fire Island vacation encased in a crisp outer layer of calamine lotion and bandages ("like Claude Rains in *The Invisible Man*") due to a case of poison ivy he had contracted near the Ocean Beach Inn, there was no plausible way in which a silver lining could be uncovered.

When Perelman took the obligatory voyage to Europe in 1927, this adventure was a disappointment as well. Although he managed to avoid contracting poison ivy and did manage to bear back from the Continent a copy of the "sacred text," *Ulysses* (Prohibition prohibited more than alcohol in those days), he had failed to find the adventures and atmosphere in his Berlin and Paris pilgrimages that movies and books had led him to expect. Instead of the fascinating intrigues promised by an Emil Jannings film called *Variety*, Berlin's Wintergarten cabaret entertained its patrons with accordionists and third-rate magicians. And Paris was not really peopled with Lady Bretts and Jake Barneses as depicted in *The Sun Also Rises*, but with other literary voyeurs who had come to the Dôme, the Select, and the Closerie-des-Lilas in a wild-goose chase after literary phantoms, too, just as Perelman had. Like all of Perelman's voyages after the exotic promised him on celluloid or the printed page, this first European trip signalled that reality was always going to prove a good deal more obvious and tiresome than the daydreams of escapist art. But if disappointment is a comic writer's stock-in-trade, the man behind the writer feels just the way the rest of us do about disappointment. And by this point, Perelman's own prophetic wall was by now crowded with handwriting. By about 1929, four wretched years after graduation, it was becoming clear to him that he "was not destined to be another Ingres or Delacroix,"[26] or even a passable professional cartoonist. And so, like many another young man who finds his first dreams about himself fallen on stoney ground, Perelman reaffirmed his identity by securing himself to someone who knew him for his real worth. On July 4, 1929, he was married to Laura West, Nathanael West's sister, "a bold-eyed, willowy brunette who had been scanning me as a matrimonial prospect for some time."[27] Paris was a natural choice for the honeymoon.

Marriage marked the close of the Left Bank period of Perelman's career. For four years he had subsisted on crullers and incense, endured avant-gardist cant in coffeehouses, and suffered his cartoons and erotic advances to be rejected. He had indeed made some headway as a writer, but a journal that was to be called *Mickey Finn*, conceived of as an American version of *Simplicissimus* (the German satirical magazine of the 1920s), had died in embryo in 1927, forestalling Perelman's uncertain drift toward an anti-Establishment forum. All he recalled from his night classes in drawing at the Art Students' League was the dictum, "Ladies and gentlemen, the breast is a cage"[28] and the feel of charcoal "maddeningly" crumbling in his fingers. Still, he did have his words. As he modestly puts it, "I drifted into writing, principally because my cartoon captions became longer and longer and longer."[29]

In his *Annus Mirabile* of 1929, Perelman not only got married, but he also published his first collection of short prose pieces, *Dawn Ginsbergh's Revenge*. Horace Liveright brought the book out, "a curious little volume, bound in the horripilating green plush used to upholster railroad chairs."[30] Throwing out a lifeline to the future, it bore on its dust jacket praise for Perelman solicited from Groucho Marx: "From the moment I picked up your book until I laid it down, I was convulsed with laughter. Someday I intend reading it." Enthusiasts of the classic Perelman are usually startled to see how very conventional are these early pieces from *Judge* and *College Humor*. For example, one bit is called "The Complete Speech-Maker: A Manual of Elegant and Appropriate Replies for Every Occasion" and includes some rhetorical flourishes one can use on the parents when expelled from college for shooting craps. Awkwardly broadcasting his literary enthusiasms, Perelman calls a tramp steamer the *Max Beerbohm* and labels a town "Mencken, Massachusetts"; and he indulges himself in a bit of embarrassing mock-naughtiness by claiming he bartered a cartoon to *Judge* in return for "the last forty pages of *Ulysses*"—that is, for the juiciest sequences of Molly Bloom's soliloquy. The wisecracks are usually near-misses, too: "There is no such person as Calvin Coolidge." The whole performance is brittle, nervous, and undergraduate, and the wit lacks the confidence and tact we associate with the great comic writing of Swift, Twain, Joyce, Ring Lardner, Salinger, or Nabokov—or S. J. Perelman.

In March 1929, just before his marriage, Perelman was obliquely involved in the genesis of West's bleak and brilliant fable, *Miss Lonelyhearts*. West was then working as an assistant manager at the Kenmore Hall Hotel on East 23rd Street in order to keep body and soul together while attempting to write his way to fame and fortune, and one night Perelman dropped by with a suggestion that they go to dinner at Siegel's, a Village restaurant the two of them frequented. At the suggestion of an acquaintance who wrote for the *Brooklyn Eagle*, Perelman had arranged to look over some letters which she had received from readers of an advice-and-agony column that appeared under her pseudonym, "Susan Chester." The woman felt that Perelman might be able to use the letters for comic mulch, but they were of course far too vulnerable and earnestly pathetic for his style: as Jay Martin puts it, "Perelman's point of view [is] brilliantly designed to puncture pretension in all its forms,"[31] and the letters were a sort of clumsy folk-poetry at once beneath and beyond pretension, their appeals to "Susan Chester" painfully literal and hopelessly sincere. But from the first moment he laid eyes on the letters, West intuitively recognized their appropriateness to his genius, for to him they encapsulated a tragic world glimpsed through a very thin veneer of unintentional comedy. Although Perelman was to find *Miss Lonely-*

hearts "too psychological, not concrete enough"[32] when he read the first portion of the manuscript, West's book came out in 1933 and remains one of the most haunting and highly regarded of contemporary American novels.

After returning from their Paris honeymoon, Perelman and Laura moved into an apartment near Washington Square, where they felt like immigrants and parvenus: "The only qualifications for residence in this landmark were a six-generation listing in the Social Register, a diploma from Groton or Miss Hewitt's classes, and eleven million dollars."[33] But money and connections are not everything. Along with West, the Perelmans saw more than a little of America's most interesting literary milieu. College classmates like Quentin Reynolds and I. J. Kapstein were then part of New York's large crowd of journalists and editors, and bohemian poets like Maxwell Bodenheim, just beginning his slide into alcoholism and poverty, at least provided local color. Perelman met Philip Wylie, with whose satirical eye he had affinities, and he would soon begin to publish alongside many distinguished writers in the *New Yorker*, the magazine Harold Ross had created in 1925. The *New Yorker* was in fact so successful that it had quickly hurried off with the circulation, readership, advertising revenue, and talent that had accumulated around *Judge* ("The World's Wittiest Weekly") and the "old" *Life* (a humor magazine that sold its last asset, its name, to Henry Luce in 1936, for $92,000). But if the *New Yorker* lured writers from its rival magazines, Hollywood would soon poach that same talent from the *New Yorker*—it is startling to realize that no fewer than ten of the magazine's original advisory editors became screenwriters, including Charles Brackett, Robert Benchley, Dorothy Parker, Nunnally Johnson, and the man who would eventually produce the two Marx brothers movies Perelman worked on, Herman J. Mankiewicz. In fact, the Marx brothers connection and his sojourn in Hollywood were to highlight the next phase in Perelman's career.

Monkey Business

"I did two films with them, which in its way is perhaps my greatest distinction in life, because anybody who ever worked on any picture for the Marx Brothers said he would rather be chained to a galley oar and lashed at ten-minute intervals until the blood spurted from his frame than ever work for those sons of bitches again,"[34] Perelman would claim after the (movie) shooting stopped. But he himself initiated the famous partnership with high hopes and hero worship.

In 1930, the Marx Brothers were just finishing an extremely successful two and a half year Broadway run in their show *Animal Crackers*, but at that point in their careers they were undecided whether to try a turn in London or perhaps to move on to radio. Perelman and Laura attended one of the performances of *Animal Crackers* and he sent a note of praise backstage to Groucho "billowing with huzzahs and hosannas"[35] and no doubt recalling with rose-tinted nostalgia the Keith-Albee in Providence and the battered canvases of *Home Again*. After a short meeting with his admirer, Groucho felt that Perelman might well be just the wordsmith to fashion a radio script for the brothers Marx, and he contacted another writer-cartoonist he knew, Will Johnstone of the old *New York Evening World*, to help Perelman work up a trial script. The prospectus the two of them flogged into shape included, for no good reason, a sketch concerning some stowaways on an ocean liner, but Perelman felt such grave reservations about the whole outline that he expected to be "pistol-whipped and summarily flung into Times Square." Groucho, however, was delighted: "This isn't any fly-by-night radio script—it's our next picture."[36]

It almost wasn't. Perelman's euphoria, his feeling of having stumbled on "The Lost Dutchman Mine," lasted at least until he entrained for Hollywood courtesy of Jesse Lasky of Paramount Pictures, who signed Perelman and Johnstone to weekly contracts and sent them west to finish the script. Perelman brought Laura and a schnauzer; Johnstone brought his comic strip and three stone crocks of illegal apple jack. For six weeks the writers labored away amid thirty or forty other Hollywood writers "in a ramshackle warren of tan stucco" on the Paramount lot. But the Marxes were being very well received in London (half a century before Monty Python), and, perhaps out of a sudden giddy contempt for New York and all its offspring, cabled Lasky to fire Perelman and Johnstone. Lasky ignored the cable but made sure his two charges knew the Marxes had sent it—writers threatened with unemployment tend to be a good deal less uppity than writers with long-term contracts.

Herman Mankiewicz had warned Perelman and Johnstone that their work for the brothers would be "an ordeal by fire. Make sure you wear your asbestos pants,"[37] and on February 20, 1931, Perelman and Johnstone were to test the temperature of the brimstone by reading the 126-page script to the clan. The writers were, of course, nervous, but they figured they had a good script—at least it had amused *them*. In order to make it all sound officially filmic, though, they inserted into their concoction every bit of cinematic arcana they could scrape up: irises, pans, tilts, dissolves, Jackman shots, Dunning shots, even going so far as to invent the transitive verb "to vorkapick"—Slavko Vorkapich was a film editor and theorist of the time—although they had no idea what the term indicated or whether or not you could do it with a 35mm camera.

For some reason or other, the crucial reading was to take place in a conference room in the Los Angeles Roosevelt Hotel. The flip of a coin decided that Perelman would read their script aloud, and although he had confidence in the material—he and Johnstone had been capsizing themselves with their own hilarious gags back at the studio sweatshop—he had grave reservations about his own capabilities as an oral narrator; indeed, other than the Classical High debating team, his "only Thespian flight heretofore had been a minor role in a . . . pageant based on Pocahontas."[38] Herman Mankiewicz was the first to arrive to hear the script read and he was forty-five minutes late. His brother Joseph (screenwriter for *All About Eve* and *A Letter to Three Wives*) accompanied him, and Perelman and Johnstone were further perplexed to find themselves confronting such savvy filmland professionalism. But at least the Mankiewiczes were *human*: Zeppo Marx arrived with his wife and a pair of frisky Afghan hounds (whose frisk quotient had been raised by an afternoon ingestion of automobile upholstery). Harpo arrived with a pair of blondes he had picked up somewhere, and Chico arrived with his wife, whose wirehair terrier immediately started a fight with the Afghans. Groucho and his own wife finally arrived, accompanied by veteran vaudeville-Hollywood gagmen Arthur Sheekman, Nat Perrin, and a cartoonist named J. Carver Pusey whom Harpo had hired to write sight-gags for him—

Pusey's strip, "Little Benny," concerned a boy who could not talk.
Even "Frenchy" Marx, the family paterfamilias, showed up with a
pinochle buddy. Various and sundry Paramount officials had gotten
wind of the reading, too, so when Perelman quavered into the first
lines of the first draft of *Monkey Business* the audience consisted of no
less than twenty-seven people and five dogs, and the Marxes had just
gotten into Los Angeles after four days on a transcontinental train.

Sheekman later said that Perelman's reading was both miserable
and valiant in equal measure. "I would have shot myself on page
twenty-five."[39] For ninety minutes Perelman droned on, "like a
Hindu chanting the Bhagavad-Gita,"[40] and of course the performance
was a total frost.

"What do you think?" Chico asked Groucho at the conclusion of
Perelman's ordeal.

"It stinks," Groucho said without hesitation, and everyone in the
room, human and canine alike, hastened to agree.

Having written a bad script in the golden age of Hollywood was
not quite the same as failing, though—quite otherwise. Because the
script was so inferior, Perelman and Johnstone were not fired, they
were put on salary for the next five months to work up something
filmable. The experience continued to a lucrative ordeal. "It took
drudgery and Homeric quarrels, ambuscades and intrigues that would
have shamed the Borgias," Perelman recalls of the production process. Everyone seemed to have a bright idea, but no two bright ideas
seemed to go together. "Every day the shouting, bargaining, impro-
vising, compromising, and mob warfare would continue," as Joe
Adamson put it. The two main combatants were producer Mankiewicz
and writer Sheekman. Sheekman wanted a plot, but Mankiewicz
claimed that "if Groucho and Chico stand against a wall for an hour
and forty minutes and crack funny jokes, that's enough of a plot for
me." They struck a compromise, and *Monkey Business* was made
without a plot.

It does have a situation, though: the Marx brothers stow away on
an ocean liner and a good many complications inevitably arise from
that deception. The movie is really a cartoon with people. Like all
cartoons, the essence of this one is a chase. From the opening moments, when they jack-in-the-box up from four barrels of kippered

herring, the Marxes are a study in maniacal *chutzpah*, "ruthless gnomes from another realm" who attack the pulpy gray routines, ceremonies, and conventions of life aboard ship with gleeful aggressiveness and a "mood of unabated rebellion and out-and-out revolt," as Adamson puts it.

Director Norman McLeod held things together just long enough to put the action on celluloid. A university light-heavyweight boxing champ and a fighter pilot in World War I, the agreeable McLeod was the only person who seemed to be able to organize all the nonsense into something resembling a movie. "I'm as quiet as a mouse pissing on a blotter,"[41] he used to say, but those quiet tones carried real authority, and on release in late 1931 the movie proved itself a resounding hit. It has since risen from a hit to a classic.

"Considering it was just about everybody's first movie, it had no right turning out so good, " Joe Adamson notes of *Monkey Business*. Perelman's contributions—the "esoteric literary dialogue" he fought with Sheekman and others to include—can readily be discerned in Groucho's repartee. For example, when the gangster Alky Briggs tells Groucho, "I'm wise! I'm wise!" Groucho's reply is, "You're wise, eh? Well, what's the capital of Nebraska? What's the capital of the Chase Manhattan Bank? Give up?" When the ship's captain threatens to throw him in irons, Grouch replies that "You can't do it with irons, it's a mashie shot. It's a mashie shot if the wind's against you, and if the wind isn't against you, I am!"[42]

Although Groucho is really the only American comedian ever known for his quick sallies and clever, epigrammatic use of words, he became one of the many who have accused Perelman's comedy writing as being too purely verbal for the stage or screen. Interviewed for *Take One* in 1970, Groucho's acerbity also revealed that their long friendship was under a real strain at the time, although the two of them tried to publicly patch things up before Groucho died in 1977. Asked if Perelman had not written for the Marx brothers, Groucho replied that the humorist's contributions to their careers had been very slight: "When he was riding high on the *New Yorker*, and anybody asked him if he'd worked with the Marx Brothers, he'd say, 'A little bit, not very much.' Now that he isn't so successful any more, and his name isn't front page, when he gives an interview he says, 'Oh yes, I wrote pretty near all of two of their movies,' which is a goddamned lie. . . . He wasn't a dramatist. He could write funny dialogue, but that's very different from writing drama."[43] Quite possibly Groucho was reacting to the sort of interview in which Perelman would describe the brothers as "treacherous to a degree that would make Machiavelli absolutely kneel at their feet,"[44] but the claim that Perelman's best effects come across with more verve on the printed page than from the lips of an actor is hardly arguable. Although family loyalty might have colored his judgment, Groucho's son Arthur made a statement in his memoir about his father and uncles that contains a home truth: "S. J. Perelman was better than many [of their screenwriters], but he fell into the same trap. He mistook tongue-twisting repartee and high-flown hyperbole for genuine humor, and zany scenes for identifiable situations. . . . His humor is better read than heard."[45] All of Perelman's efforts for the stage and screen suffer from this problem; he is a reader's writer, not a writer for audiences who must watch and listen.

Not a Marxist

Aside from the difficulty of working with the Marxes themselves and the hectic, noisy, *ad hoc* atmosphere that seemed essential to their creation, Perelman's sensibility did not fit into their comic world very well.

In an excellent article on Perelman and Nathanael West and their relationship to Hollywood, J. A. Ward makes a point at once significant and subtle. Ward describes the Marxes in their comic roles as "irreverent and destructive eccentrics" who attack not just ordinary society in its everyday moments, but the "theatrical productions of society"—that is, they attack society when it is most pompous, most stylized, when it is celebrating itself at the right-fork dinner, or at the opera, or in the social rituals peculiar to transatlantic voyages: society when it is most purely society.

The Marxes convert these social rituals and stylized theatricals into "back-alley capers," and in the process "the lowly is exalted, the lofty is trivialized." The Marxes, then, are to some extent satisfying because they are figures of social anger, of comic subversion; they are outsiders and underdogs who convert the social formulae of the Establishment into a shambles, and when we laugh at their antics we are enjoying a comic and bloodless form of class warfare. The Marx brothers are Marxists.

And we are asked to admire them. In this war, they are ruthless, as invulnerable as the mice gangs of animated cartoons, and relentlessly physical. But as Ward points out, Perelman's comic persona is not an anarchist or guerilla-fighter in full attack on false conventions and papier-mâché pretense, he is a "hyper-literary naive" who frequently and through clear fault of his own, "becomes entrapped into actual or quasi-show business situations dominated by manic tyrants." In Perelman's world, the Groucho figures are not heroes of social insurgency, but "leaders of the establishment, the movie moguls and department-store entrepreneurs whose bravado and unscrupulousness are at the service of fakery. It is to the point . . . that Perelman despised the Marx Brothers and took little pleasure in writing for them."[46]

Looking back over almost fifty years of his work, we can confidently generalize a little about Perelman's comic persona. He has every minor vice and defect except stupidity: he is vain (with little to be vain about), lecherous (although usually unsuccessful in his pursuit of the ladies), greedy, slothful, and a braggart. He is never presented as being adept at anything, including his transgressions. Only his vocabulary and perceptions really separate him from the grosser clowns and con-men whose success he desires for himself. Although he is a victim, like Chaplin's Little Tramp, he is never innocent, or at least completely innocent. He is a shlemiel, but an aware shlemiel, never a passive victim. He shares with W. C. Fields a touch of petty knavery, but he is more impulsive than cynical and far more naive than knavish. Like Falstaff, he knows full well the better part of valor, and like Falstaff he is swollen with high-flown rhetoric to disguise it; in his asides to us he is frequently a realist, but in front of his fellows he is nine parts puffery and one part fraud. If Perelman's persona should ever be written up for use in a movie, the part should be played by Don Knotts—with a thesaurus in his pocket. None of the Marx brothers embodies this sort of comic persona, and after helping write up the script for *Horsefeathers* in 1931 (this time in collaboration with two old Marxian standbys and script doctors from their vaudeville days, Bert Kalmar and Harry Ruby), Perelman never worked with the brothers again: the sigh of the relief must have been large, heartfelt, and mutual.

Although Perelman said that "writing *Horsefeathers* was easy, pleasant work, comparable to shaving with a piece of glass or removing a coat of tar and feathers,"[47] the sequel to *Monkey Business* is actually more congenial with Perelman's interests—lighter and less aggressive. Groucho plays a professor called Quincey Adams Wagstaff who is suddenly (and for no reason at all) elevated to the presidency of Huxley College and, as Nabokov used to say to his literature classes, "Well, you can see the possibilities." Chico is a bootlegger, Harpo is a dogcatcher, and Zeppo is a student courting the college widow: in other words, the plot is a series of unconnected sketches and gags, with the film occasionally reminding itself to include a mild sort of satire on owlish academic solemnity and self-importance. The professors even wear their academic robes, and they all seem to have flowing white beards in the manner of medieval schoolmen; as Joe Adamson says, the movie's idea of a college professor "must rank somewhere between Captain Hook and the Sheriff of Nottingham on the believability charts."[48] At what is alleged to be a faculty meeting, Groucho sings to them a song that became famous enough to be cited in disparagement of the Students for a Democratic Society and its ilk during the student rebellions in the Vietnam era: "Whatever it is, I'm Against It." Perelman's hand might be detected in Groucho's comebacks and one-liners; for example, when Groucho threatens to dismantle the dormitories, he is asked where the students would sleep. Answer: "Where they always sleep. In the classroom." There is a climactic football sequence the plagiarization of which Perelman had no hand in—Kalman and Ruby were no doubt inspired by a famous sequence in Harold Lloyd's *The Freshman*. The film suffers from the lack of a central chase-creating mechanism like the stowaway gimmick in *Monkey Business*, though, and it seems to many commentators and *cineastés* to be "forced" and "inadequate." Britain's *New Statesman* found its sketches "a series of culs-de-sac," but Marx brothers enthusiasts like Allen Eyles prefer it to *Monkey Business*, whose wordplay and erudition is "more for minority tastes."[49] In any event, Perelman's filmwriting career was set into motion, once and for all. The results would be painful for him, delightful for us. As Perelman himself has said, misery breeds copy.

The Hollywood Sargasso

Everyone agrees that Hollywood is a city of magic, but to some who have worked there the color of that magic is the inkiest black. Perelman loathed the place. It was to him "a dreary industrial town controlled by hoodlums of enormous wealth, the ethical sense of a pack of jackals, and taste so degraded that it befouled everything it touched."[50] Not that he was above taking their money, of course: from 1931 through 1942, Perelman and Laura periodically journeyed to the Coast to "replenish the larder,"[51] but they were scrupulous to return East after each lucrative project. It was a wise and admirable policy to keep that larder out of California. Unlike the Algonquin group, Perelman would rent his talent to the moguls of celluloid, but never sell it to them outright, and those "hoodlums of enormous wealth" would have been very happy to have locked away that talent behind the studio door along with all the other Eastern, Algonquin, and Ivy League wits who had surrendered so easily to the easy money and endless sunshine and decided to stay on forever. Selling out for large amounts of the filthy stuff is always easy, of course, and the list of Eastern writers who became kept talents in Hollywood is a distinguished one: Dorothy Parker, Donald Ogden Stewart, and Robert Benchley from the *New Yorker*, all of whom Perelman loyally claims had "no more connections with the screen-writing fraternity than if they'd been Martians;"[52] Nunnally Johnson, who wrote more than one hundred scripts; Marc Connelly of *The Green Pastures* fame; and of course, Herman Mankiewicz, Columbia University '16, who while producing W. C. Fields's *Million-Dollar Legs* and the Marxes' *Monkey Business* and *Horsefeathers* (and before he went on to help Orson Welles write the screenplay for *Citizen Kane* and achieve at least a cult immortality) pointed out in exasperation that "the part-time help of wits is no better than the full-time help of half-wits."[53]

Perelman's help was most definitely of the part-time variety, and he was merely one more pencil-pusher among the 1,275 who toiled away on the studio lots in those boom-town days of movie production, when so many people escaped the Great Depression by way of the silver screen (world-wide admissions amounted to 2.8 billion customers in 1933, the worst year of the economic crisis).

Although he likes to denigrate the concept of film production with images from the dreary, repetitious world of the factory (Perelman speaks of his writing for the movies as approximately as inspiring as turning out piece-work on a shoe lathe "in Lynn, Massachusetts"), a more vivid metaphor—because richer in connotations of wastefulness, inertia, and decay—is the comment he made to George Plimpton: Hollywood immobilized and then swallowed talent whole, and in the 1930s, when the only rich writers were writers for the screen, Perelman claimed the film industry "resembled the Sargasso Sea—an immense, turgidly revolving whirlpool in which literary hulks encrusted with verdigris moldered until they sank."[54] Determined that he would not vanish into this Bermuda Triangle of lost talent, Perelman simply wrote the stuff required by the studios, cashed his checks, and kept his aesthetic and ethical bearings by looking back toward the East. For him, writing for the movies was an "occupation which, like herding swine, makes the vocablualry pungent but contributes little to one's prose style"(M, 1). But of course the Hollywood scene would furnish him with a wealth of comic and satiric possibilities for his prose.

The archetypal film director Rouben Mamoulian was supposed to have said that "the picture industry is no different from the underwear business," and the archetypal film tyrant Harry Cohn of Columbia Pictures is on record as declaring "It's not a business, it's a racket!" Although these utterances are a sort of irrefutable folk-poetry and faultlessly true as far as they go, two very gifted writers, one American, one British, expressed the eerie and disquieting truth about Hollywood in a pair of statements that I find even more interesting, accurate, and deadly.

In his notes for the uncompleted manuscript of The Last Tycoon, F. Scott Fitzgerald pointed out that the "better men" had soon been eliminated from the picture-making business "from the needs of speed," and that in the gold-rush atmosphere of the place there had been an emphasis on the "lower virtues"—tenacity, energy, survival instinct, quickness—at the expense of those virtues we would associate with the master craftsman. As a result, the picture-creating population that remained was at once coarse and yet fabulously successful, with all its artistic impulses eliminated by Darwinian selection or hidden away by conscious acts of self-suppression. Further, the men that were left were all part of an industry that they could claim to have helped make an extravagant success, "despite the fact that not a third of the producers or one-twentieth of the writers could have earned their living in the East. There was not one of those no matter how low-grade or incompetent a fellow, who could not claim to have participated largely in success. This made difficulty in dealing with them."[55]

The second quote is from Evelyn Waugh, a writer who loathed the motion-picture industry almost as intensely as did Perelman, and who came to write the most savagely hilarious of all anti-Hollywood novels, *The Loved One*. Speaking of Fitzgerald himself, Waugh noted in his diary that "The enormously expensive apparatus of the film studio can produce nothing as valuable as can one half-tipsy Yank with a typewriter."[56] (On his visit to Hollywood, Waugh felt that after he had met Charlie Chaplin and visited the Disney Studios, he had "paid homage to the two artists of the place.") Perelman would no doubt co-sign these insights: he immediately saw that it was the nature of the movie business to turn the individual talent into a hired hand.

His own taste in movies ran to "swifty, witty pictures" like *The Thin Man* series with William Powell and Myrna Loy, or Billy Wilder's *Double Indemnity* (written by another kept Easterner and *New Yorker* contributor, Charles Brackett), or James Cagney giving off sparks as the crime czar Tom Powers in *Public Enemy*. But Perelman did not get to work on the really good ones, the ones with personality and snap. In the thirties the movies were what television is today, a mass-produced commodity, the kind of undifferentiated pop cult that ran along the iron grooves of genre: "mother love, Navy heroics, and canine loyalty,"[57] as Perelman puts it. And many bright ideas came to nothing at all. For example, Perelman once labored for twenty-two weeks with three different sets of collaborators—one set a pair of veteran hacks who specialized in gangster films, another a brace of young idealists who tried to introduce social conscience into every frame—on a project to bring Cole Porter's *Nymph Errant* to the screen. Nothing came of it. Another stillborn effort was a bizarre attempt to work up a script for Dale Carnegie's *How To Win Friends and Influence People* as a vehicle for Joan Crawford and Fanny Brice, but this at least brought Perelman together with Ogden Nash with happy consequences for both of them later. Perelman confesses that the two of them "did not attend strictly to our knitting,"[58] while they were captives together in the studio sweatshops, and he claims that the only result of all the time and money that went into the project was a Sherlock Holmes trivia quiz he and Nash cooked up for their own amusement. He also labored on "a loathesome little thing called *Greenwich Village*" (after all, he had lived in Greenwich Village, hadn't he?), another unsuccessful attempt to create a vehicle for Joan Crawford. MGM blew $75,000 on this one. In 1934 he and Laura were able to at least get something on the screen, and it was a film in which they had invested their own experience, too. The movie was *Paris Interlude*.

Paris Interlude began life as a play the Perelmans wrote together called *All Good Americans*—one of Oscar Wilde's carved-ivory epigrams claims that all good Americans go to Paris when it's time for them to die. The play opened on December 6, 1933, just as Prohibition sloshed to a close, and ran for forty performances at Henry Miller's Theatre before it, too, closed. The reviews were unflattering. Brooks Atkinson, whose Jehovah-voice from the *Times* almost always spelled life or death for anything brought to Broadway, described it as a "second-rate Philip Barry comedy,"[59] one after which "you have to scratch your head to remember the jokes." The plot is ancient and eternal boy-meets-girl business: Julie Gable, a fashion writer, falls in love with Pat Wells, an amiable barfly. After losing her, Pat wins her hand in marriage, and the curtain coming down signifies happily ever after. The mise-en-scène concerns a group of relentlessly sophisticated Americans living in Paris, and the dialogue consists of that unconvincing wiseacre stuff that hopes to pass itself off as champagne but really tastes like 3.2 beer: for example, when a simpering college girl complains in standard stage drawl that back in school "we had the *best coffee*," nothing like this French stuff, she is blasted into the outer darkness with this riposte: "Where did you go to school? Maxwell House?"

The Perelmans' bookish concerns pop up in one-liners that now require footnotes; for example, Michael Arlen, an Armenian immigrant to America, had written a famous best-selling novel of the period called *The Green Hat*, and he is gigged with a somewhat labored in-joke. An Armenian rug dealer is trundled out into the action for the sole purpose of having Pat tell him that "I like *The Green Hat* all right, but that last book of yours was terrible." *All Good Americans* also contains a biographical touch invisible to the uninformed eye. The Perelmans had actually fostered a romance between Nathanael West and Beatrice Mathieu, then the fashion correspondent for the *New Yorker*, during the time that Beatrice had been brought back to the magazine's Manhattan offices under Harold Ross's standing policy for his overseas correspondents. The Perelmans had met her during their 1929 Parisian honeymoon and hoped to make a suitable match for West, but the incipient romance seems to have foundered in that storm-tossed inland sea we often seem to find within young writers still trying to find themselves and whose commitment to art lashes furiously against the bourgeois practicalities of supporting a wife.

Andre Senwald of the *New York Times* wrote that "it is impossible not to like *Paris Interlude* a little, though the film doesn't really deserve it,"[60] and this sort of left-handed near-praise was evidently enough to encourage the film industry to keep on wiring for the Perelmans to come out to the Coast and cobble together yet another script. In fact, Nathanael West's career as a Hollywood screenwriter—he worked on no fewer than twenty-eight different projects before his death in an automobile accident in 1940—was in part a result of Perelman's encouragement as to the ease of getting hold of some of the money the studios seemed so anxious to give away: "Don't worry about clichés and familiar situations, you can go to enough movies to see what kind of fare they dole out," Perelman wrote West, and the man who was to be the author of *Day of the Locust* (1939) soon found himself out in a southern California that Edmund Wilson described for his Eastern brethren in letters as composed of "brown papier mâché hills where every prospect appeases and the goofs hang like ripe fruit."[61] The astonishing nature of Hollywood reality summoned from West the novel many observers feel is the best expression of that conscienceless brutality and childish irresponsibility that we have come to associate with the noun "Hollywood."

In 1936 both Perelmans adapted a short story by Clarence B. Kelland ("Recreation Car") into a movie called *Florida Special*, a humdrum production centering on a gem theft, complete with Jack Oakie as a newspaperman with his fedora pushed to the back of his head and Sidney Blackmer oozing cultivated evil as the villain.

Perelman felt his low-point as a scenarist was his collaboration on "a pestilence called *Sweethearts*" for Nelson Eddy and Jeanette MacDonald, the infamous singing duo "whose archness made toes curl"[62] all over the Western world, and who were known to the denizens of Hollywood's literary subculture as "The Singing Capon" and "The Iron Butterfly."

In 1939 the Perelmans wrote a script called *Ambush*, a crime film Paramount brought out that year. Even though the piece had been initiated merely as a vehicle for an ex-Metropolitan Opera soprano named Gladys Swarthout, the reviews were good. Bosley Crowther appreciated the fact that the Perelman touch added "just enough comic by-play to keep it unmistakably within the bounds of purest fiction, [and it is] lively, amusing stuff."[63] *Newsweek*'s anonymous reviewer said that "Robert Hay's story has been transformed by Laura and S. J. Perelman into a taut, suspenseful script which, under Kent Neumann's direction, is notable for its imaginative detail and lack of melodramatic clichés."[64] Those are pretty good notices, and the Perelmans could easily have spent the rest of their careers in Hollywood turning out toy screenplays. It is important to remember that most writers with their opportunities, achievements, and connections did just that. But if Perelman would never admit to any virtues, it is our obligation to pin at least one on him: artistic integrity.

MGM brought out a turkey called *The Golden Fleecing* in 1940, and Perelman and five other screenwriters were accused of allowing their collective comic muse to go "wool-gathering"[65] while the film was made—the *Times* reviewer, Theodore Strauss, evidently thought that a good many comic possibilities had been missed. The plot, no doubt palsied with senility even by this time, centered around the efforts of an insurance salesman (Lew Ayres) to protect the life of a gangster with a price on his head to whom he had just sold a large policy.

The last film Perelman was to write before Mike Todd coaxed him back to Hollywood in the mid-1950s to win the Academy Award for *Around the World in Eighty Days* was an adaptation of his and Laura's play *The Night Before Christmas*, yet another crime comedy.

The Night Before Christmas had scored a minor success on the legitimate stage (twenty-one performances at New York's Morosco), but Brooks Atkinson had noticed something vital missing from its structure when he reviewed it for the *Times*: it was, he said, an "incomplete comedy,"[66] and definitely "not one of the most hilarious escapades of the season"; and of course the sparkle of Perelman's *New Yorker* prose had led him to expect better things. The basic gimmick sounds like fairly good box office, though. A pair of incompetent safecrackers discover a luggage store on Manhattan's Sixth Avenue that is for sale, and next door to the luggage shop stands a bank. The safecrackers buy the luggage store in order to tunnel through into the adjacent vaults while the bank is closed for the Christmas holidays, but of course the luggage shop's customers keep getting in the way. Atkinson points out that the piece "never accumulates a story that develops out of normal life into comic fantastification" (another charge frequently leveled at Perelman's stage and screen work), but when the play was redone as a movie and released as *Larceny, Inc.* by Warner Brothers in 1942, Edward G. Robinson, already beginning to parody his own gangster persona, managed to make the story "very hectic and amusing."[67] And Perelman made a tidy $30,000 on the movie sale.

Saint Thalberg

Of all the sainted names from the Golden Age of Hollywood, Irving Thalberg's is the most bloated with pseudo-reverence and undeserved praise. Although Thalberg was the model for the protagonist of Scott Fitzgerald's great and uncompleted novel of Hollywood, *The Last Tycoon*, Perelman has scoffed at the reverent "hush" produced at the mere mention of the producer. Nor did Thalberg's death at thirty-six (his heart had been damaged by rheumatic fever in childhood) cause

Perelman to sentimentalize the man. Thalberg had once declared with what Perelman calls "Mosaic profundity," that for the movies a writer, any writer, was only a "necessary evil," to which statement Perelman has added: "The assertion that he said 'weevil' appears to have no foundation in fact" (*M*, 599). It was Thalberg who had perfected one of the most dark, Satanic features of the Hollywood fantasy-mills, the use of writing teams, teams that were sometimes even competing with each other, and no writer of Perelman's individuality could be expected to like having his work mutilated by a series of incompetents taking turns with it—mutilation by assembly line. "I never thought that I had more brains than a writer has," Fitzgerald has his Monroe Stahr explain to a labor organizer in *The Last Tycoon*. "But I always thought that his brains *belonged* to me—because I knew how to use them."[68] In the novel we see that Stahr's attitude is finally the best one, but in Perelman's report from the front lines, reality at MGM's New Writer's Building (known to its occupants as the Neuritis and Neuralgia Building) was of course something else again.

In the first place, Perelman implies, Thalberg had no taste. That he wanted the Perelmans to write an adaptation of *Greenwich Village* was in itself preposterous: "Why, it's pure parody," Laura exclaimed after an astonished look at the novel. "He *can't* be in earnest about this . . . all these roistering poets, the painters in their picturesque smocks, that motherly old bag in the boardinghouse with the capacious bosom and the heart of gold . . ." (*M*, 600). But of course Thalberg was in earnest; MGM had already paid $75,000 for the screen rights to the book, and considerably more was spent to have other and even costlier writers attempt to create a workable screenplay out of this sow's ear.

It was perhaps the sheer wastefulness of the screenwriting factories that most appalled the Perelmans, and the *Greenwich Village* fiasco was a good example of it. With the ink on their contracts still drying (Laura had observed that writing for the movies was at least going to prove more lucrative than picking lettuce in the Imperial Valley, no matter what injury they were inflicting on the muses), an unctuous and condescending chaperone showed the two of them to their fly-blown little office on the Metro lot. Thalberg, the man told them, was "the greatest intellect we have" (*M*, 601), and a very humble and lovable human being as well. He implied that the Perelmans should count themselves lucky to be working for him.

Since the Perelmans were so obviously not in awe of Thalberg or properly dumbstruck with their good fortune, the chaperone went on to tell them that the previous occupant of their office had been a celebrated lady playwright much in vogue. The woman had spent the last fourteen months therein, in fact, but she had possessed a talent so ethereal that no story worthy of her talents could be found for her to work on in all that time. When the chaperone had finally left them to their own devices, the Perelmans found inside the office desk a "pair of highly intricate doilies, created by braiding together narrow strips of yellow typewriting paper"—the only memento of the lady play-wright's incarceration there. Perelman swiftly calculated that if she had been salaried at the rate of, say, $1,500 a week, those doilies had cost the studio about $84,000, "A heart-warming example of crafts-manship adequately rewarded" (*M*, 601). Still, the Perelmans were going to discover that those doilies were one of the few tangible accomplishments ever achieved within the confines of the battered and dirty little office, and the objects began to take on the mute eloquence of graffiti carved into the walls of a medieval dungeon.

Thalberg ignored his new writing team, just as he had the lady playwright, and the Perelmans felt that they ought not to begin their adaptation until they found out what he had in mind. A week passed, then a month. Six weeks. The Perelmans' agent told them to relax, endorse those checks, and wait. This was the depression, they were lucky to have work. And so Laura did some needlepoint while Perelman read Boswell and worked on chess problems and watched a veteran screenwriter across the hall, Talbot Jennings, dictate the script of *Mutiny on the Bounty* into an Ediphone while having his scalp vibrated with a motorized device that resembled a "metal cocktail shaker." Nor were they consoled to learn from other phantoms around the Triangle Shirtwaist Factory[69] that Thalberg put everyone on hold, even famous playwrights earning bone-cracking salaries. They were told that time moved at a geological pace for the MGM writer, and they had better get used to it. It was not for nothing that the settee in Thalberg's antechamber was known locally as the "Mil-lion Dollar Bench."

After nine weeks and out of simple ennui, the Perelmans began to write the screenplay, visualizing Joan Crawford acting out every cliché. Now, and entirely by coincidence, the telephone summoned them to the executive offices at MGM's "College of Cardinals," and they were given an appointment with Thalberg, whom Perelman had come to suspect might be merely a local "solar myth or a deity concocted by the front office to garner prestige" (M, 603). In an enormous office obviously designed to intimidate mere earthlings with the majesty of his command, Thalberg, a "frail gentleman with intense eyes," asked them a rather foolish question about whether the heroine of *Greenwich Village* should tell her fiancé about her "premarital indiscretions." He made a little vexatious frown as he did so. Since the Perelmans had not even noticed indiscretion-telling as an element in the novel in the first place, a nervous and embarrassed silence momentarily prevented them from replying. Just then the meeting, already dying from lack of oxygen, was ended forever by the voice of a colleague movie-mogul on the phone "calling to borrow a cupful of proxies," with this call immediately followed by the phoned intelligence from some spy or sycophant on stage 9 that Greta Garbo was about to undergo nervous collapse unless Irving Thalberg arrived instantly. This ended the meeting—and, their impression on Thalberg having been so negative and negligible, end of contract. The Perelmans did not return their salary checks, though—or, for that matter, the $84,000 plaited typewriter-paper doilies. But then the statute of limitations has long since expired, so now the story can be told.

Lotus Land

Stupidity, hypocrisy, and perhaps even simple cowardice were the deficiencies that Perelman loathed in the Hollywood milieu. Remember the context. The depression years were the period in our century's history when authoritarian and racist leadership advanced more rapidly in more governments than it had ever before, but the Hollywood motion picture industry, always mindful that about forty percent of its revenues came from overseas markets, pretended that it had not noticed. Apart from Charlie Chaplin's *The Great Dictator*, no significant films were made concerning the Nazi and Fascist leaders who were soon to make war on the rest of the world. In order to avoid offending Franco and his world-wide sympathizers, no film was made at that time that took sides in the civil war in Spain; even Hemingway's *For Whom the Bell Tolls* was not made until 1943—long past the moment when its theme might have forewarned the West of Fascist brutality or Communist cynicism. The invasion of Manchuria, the first step in Japan's conquest of the Pacific world for its "Greater East Asia Co-Prosperity Sphere," did not find its way onto film until after Pearl Harbor. In Russia, the Stalinist purges, show trials, and labor camps were exposing that Great Experiment in human values for the enormous and ghastly political pogrom it really was. No film reflected that reality. Rabbis were washing the cobblestones of Nuremberg and Jewish merchants were beaten by Brownshirt thugs as early as the mid-1930s, but American movies presented us with Katharine Hepburn as a Delightfully Dizzy Debutante or Wallace Beery as a punchy but lovable prizefighter in *The Champ*. One in four Americans was out of work, but *The Grapes of Wrath* was altered from an angry and quasi-revolutionary novel to a saccharine film that ends with Jane Darwell as Ma Joad telling us that the poor would be doing all right, nothing could really keep them down, and that California was not a dead end but a promised land where one lived happily ever after.

Perelman noticed and was bothered by the hypocrisy. The "noble piety of the Hollywood folks, as they immersed themselves in the plight of the migratory workers and the like, was pretty comical. One couldn't fault them for their social conscience, but when you saw the English country houses they dwelt in, the hundred-thousand dollar estancias, and the Cadillacs they drove to protest meetings, it was to laugh."[70] Hollywood was the world's greatest image-creating machine, but the movies showed us the gauziest, silliest daydreams. Poverty was what the movies allowed you to ignore. Financially, the manufacture of escapist daydreams for the masses was unarguably the right choice. Morally, it was just cowardice and greed. As Perelman wrote to Nathanael West, "There is an air of false prosperity out here that makes news of breadlines and starvation unreal."[71] But breadlines and starvation were real. Even a direct cynicism is easier for most of us to live with than a continued pretense, and the film industry was pretending. Although Perelman was never a social activist, he was always a comic artist of the first order, and the business of a comic artist is always to see the dismal difference between what is and what ought to be. In a fundamental sense, his comedy is an essentially realistic mode of perception, an illusion-puncturing one. A place like Hollywood, dedicated to the inflation of illusions in both its unreal product and with its social organization centering on sycophancy, guile, and connections could never be a comfortable milieu for anyone of integrity, individuality, and a taste for words and images properly deployed. In his eleven years in and out of Tinseltown, Perelman studied the place with fascinated revulsion, though, and if he was once to say that a psychiatrist in the movie capital must feel like a kid in a candy store,[72] a comic humorist in Hollywood will always discover a smorgasbord spread out for him there as well. We will see Perelman make use of it again and again throughout his career.

Before they moved to a large Mexican adobe-style house at 5734 Cazoux Drive in Beverly Hills—by the end of the decade Adam and Abbey Laura Perelman had been added to the family—the Perelmans stayed at a Hollywood address that is almost more myth than fact, the famous Garden of Allah apartments. Many writers would have allowed themselves to be swept off their seats with the naughty glamor of it all—but not Perelman.

Built on Sunset Boulevard by Russian-émigré silent film star Alla [sic] Nazimova when Beverly Hills was still largely ravine and goat run, the acreage had been converted into a parklike enclave of two-story tile-roofed stucco villas in the Spanish manner. The Garden of Allah soon became a sort of Kruger Wildlife Preserve for every exotic species of European, British, and Eastern celebrity when they were on the Coast making pictures. From 1928 until 1959 (when it was demolished to make way for a bank), the Garden of Allah was Hollywood's only address with even a trace of intellectual and cultural cachet. And it also savored of tabloid wickedness—so much so that it is surprising even today that no movie was ever made about it.

Robert Benchley, who lived at No. 20, "The Bear Trap," was the patron saint of the place during those Hollywood years when he was making forty-six Paramount short subject films, allowing his comic gift for prose to atrophy from neglect, and destroying himself with a lethal pharmaceutical whipsaw of Benzedrine and sleeping pills. Cole Porter, Fannie Brice, Ernest Hemingway, Laurence Olivier and Vivien Leigh, as well as every Eastern or British writer from Scott Fitzgerald on down lived there at one time or another, and Errol Flynn, who did his best to keep up his wicked, wicked ways into late middle age, used to seduce aspiring starlets alongside a swimming pool, the odd shape of which was modeled after Nazimova's "aura" as sketched by her court astrologer. But Perelman was not intrigued by the historical significance and nutty charm of the place, even though he was aware that it was the scene of a good deal of adulterous hanky-panky by the very famous—in fact, he reports that once, when a night-time fire broke out at another building nearby, the crowd that tumbled out of the Garden of Allah's villas to watch it was composed of a good many celebrities, "all officially married, but not to their present roommates."[73] A famous, but unnamed, leading man on celluloid lived at the Garden with his socialite wife, and he kept on explaining to Perelman that her succession of black eyes and fat lips was the result of falls against a birdbath. "The third time it happened I was tactless enough to ask if there was a birdbath in their villa, as I had seen none on the grounds. Our friendship curdled abruptly, which may have been providential. There were probably more black eyes where his wife's had come from."[74] So much for high living and low deeds at Tinseltown's most famous apartment address, the place playwright Jed Harris claimed "was always on the verge of being a glorified whorehouse."[75] If there were indeed orgies and saturnalias which would have "shocked Petronius out of his toga," Perelman never took part in them, even to fuel his comic prose, and the most memorable incident involving him in the life of the place was the time he entertained the Marx brothers at a dinner party and his schnauzer ate Groucho's wife's new hat. For all its aura of glamorous sin and orgiastic bacchanalia then, the Hollywood Perelman recovers for us is the domain of those sycophants who are "ever ready to cut a competitor's throat or lick a producer's boot . . . ever alert to sell out wife, child, and principle to attain the higher bracket, the fleecier polo coat, the more amorous concubine" (*M*, 319). With so much energy spent on sycophancy there was little left over for creation of any kind; Hollywood's essential laziness did not escape Perelman, either, and he characterized that somnolence once with this wonderful description of an afternoon at the Bel-Air Hotel: "an immense, weedy lethargy, reminiscent of a bankrupt miniature golf course, shrouded the premises."[76] Fundamentally, the movieland denizens lacked the energy and will to organize themselves to any purpose other than self-advancement: too much talk, too much ego, too much sunshine. For Perelman, Lotus Land was a bore.

Nor were the overpaid and undertalented celebrities of Hollywood the only problem for Perelman's "adjustment." Like West, he was appalled by the kind of transients and hopefuls who were drawn out to the city of Technicolor. As recently as 1977, a brief visit to Hollywood and Vine evoked from Perelman an even more emphatic disgust than he had experienced in the 1930s, for in our day the world's most famous intersection has been entirely taken over by porno shops, videotape peepshows, and clothing stores for transvestites "interspersed with fast-food restaurants guaranteeing instant botulism."[77] Of course, the people sluggishly circulating about in the bright California sunshine were essentially unchanged from the flotsam of the 1930s: "the same old screwballs and screwboxes—losers of beauty contests, Texas gigolos, nature fakers . . . unemployed flagellants, religious messiahs, and jailbait." For Perelman, the face of the dream-factory had remained a "satanic troglodyte" visage, and the ambiance of that famous town "an unalloyed horror . . . a hayseed's idea of the Big Apple. . . . its tawdriness is unspeakable."[78]

When they were not enjoying Hollywood, the Perelmans lived on an 83-acre farm in Bucks County, Pennsylvania, that they had bought with Nathanael West. Perelman called the place "Eight Ball" to begin with (he seems to have dubbed it "Rising Gorge" later on), and it was a large, handsome white farmhouse with a detached cottage for West's office near a sleepy little village on the Lehigh Canal called Erwinna. Perelman had not allowed his movie work to interfere with his output of prose, or with the plays and revues he was turning out at a remarkable rate. In 1930 Liveright published a novel he coauthored entitled *Parlor, Bedlam and Bath* (with his his old Brown schoolmate Quentin Reynolds, Jr.) and Chester Tattersall of the *Times* claimed that the "authors had succeeded brilliantly,"[79] while the anonymous reviewer for the *Saturday Review of Literature* said that the volume was "good, though it falls occasionally into a bog."[80] (It should always be remembered that book reviewers, who usually seem to find themselves reading three dozen of Perelman's pieces at a single sitting, sometimes sound gouty and peevish from overindulging in so much rich fare in so short a time-span.)

In the summer of 1931 Perelman's work had finally reached the Broadway stage, with the first of seven produced stage pieces opening June 1 at the Music Box Theatre. "The Third Little Show" was a revue in two acts and thirty scenes mounted as a showcase for the English comedienne Beatrice Lillie. According to the *Times* reviewer, she was superb in her sketches, which included a dimity-clad British lady informing a circle of black African heathen as to the virtues of the English tourist; she then played one of those same virtuous English tourists cheerfully slumming in Montmarte while a murder is committed at the next table; another of her sketches depicted a latecomer to the theater driving the other occupants of her row to the point of nervous breakdown. Marc Connelly, who achieved fame in 1930 with his adaptation of Roark Bradford's dialect tales into the unique Negro folk-drama *The Green Pastures*, contributed a sketch about a train passenger who gets off at Harlem's 125th Street instead of Grand Central. Perelman, anticipating the method that he would perfect for Bert Lahr in *The Beauty Part* thirty years later, created multiple roles for Ernest Truex. Truex was reported to be very funny in his "mad protean delineation of an English gentleman, a magician, and a Southern Colonel,"[81] in a sketch Perelman called "His Wedding Night." All in all, it was not a bad beginning, with the show termed "bright and knowing and generally urbane,"[82] which is more or less the flavor a New York revue ought to have. But Perelman was not always to have such luck with the stage; or even with writing for Bea Lillie.

In 1932 Perelman collaborated with Robert MacGunigle on the comic sketches for a review called *Walk a Little Faster* which ran for 119 performances at the St. James Theater. Here the *Time*'s review— it was Brooks Atkinson again—amounted to a qualified no: Atkinson found the evening "totally uninspired," more of a "long vaudeville" routine than a witty and sophisticated revue, and he claimed to be mightily disappointed because the piece used "only the surface of

the genius at its disposal."[83] Atkinson especially descried the waste of
Bea Lillie's prodigious comic gifts in sketches that were to his palate
"mostly silly," so the formula had failed this time. In a design that
would again anticipate Perelman's triumph with creating multiple
roles for Bert Lahr, Lillie was now successively (and along with much
else) Frisco Fanny, the mature rose of a Yukon whisky parlor, and a
visiting French songstress who could only condescend to an American
audience, while Bobby Clark appeared as the dictator of Russia, an
Alaskan sourdough, and Professor Peter Peckham, famous criminol-
ogist. The songs—music by Vernon Duke, lyrics by Yip Harburg—
were dismissed as a "tumid brew" even though "April in Paris" was
one of them, and *Walk a Little Faster* was never heard from again.

Perelman never had any luck with revues, those theatrical duffel-
bags into which anything and everything can be stuffed anyhow: "of
all the roads to insolvency open to my profession, entanglement in a
revue is the shortest."[84] Not that he did not keep on trying, of
course: he was the last writer in the world to make some bogus claim
about being "constitutionally averse to the crackle of greenbacks." It
was merely that Perelman and his collaborators never found the right
formula for heavier-than-air flight. In 1932 a producer Perelman
calls Poultney Kerr mesmerized a group of theatrical angels out of
$100,000 in an attempt to reproduce the lucrative success of Richard
Rodger's 1925 hit *The Garrick Gaieties*, and threw the money away on
the five-night run of a turkey called *Sherry Flip*.

Perelman had valiantly written the sketches for *Sherry Flip* on an
advance "even a Mexican migrant worker would have flouted," but
the Boston police had excised no fewer than four of the revue's
routines during tryouts on grounds of obscenity, the director could
not keep the comedians from turning the air blue with *double entendres*,
and the dance consisted of "two portentous ballets in the style known
colloquially as 'Fire in a Whorehouse.'" Perelman claims to have been
thankful that the show simply dropped through the Broadway trap-
door into the limbo awaiting all failed shows and that the people
responsible for creating it were not ruthlessly hunted down with
bloodhounds.

Each Broadway failure sent the Perelmans back to the Hollywood
celluloid mills for another profitable round of frustration and potboil-

ers, but he managed to bring out his third collection of short prose pieces, *Strictly From Hunger*, in 1937. Miriam Borgenicht in the *New Republic* thought it good stuff, although definitely so rich as to be taken only in "judicious teaspoonfuls,"[85] and the *Saturday Review of Literature* fired off a twenty-one-gun salute: "filled to the brim with a mad, uproarious humor." By 1940 Perelman had yet another collection out, *Look Who's Talking*, and the anonymous reviewer from the *Saturday Review of Literature* might as well have been Perelman himself so fulsome and rapturous was the accolades. That magazine was all for putting Olympus on alert, claiming that the "universal monarchy of wit was never very crowded; they will find no difficulty at all making room for [Perelman] there."[86] And they were right.

As the decade closed, Perelman stepped out of his role as a prose writer to host a radio quiz show on the Mutual network called "Author, Author," which had its inaugural broadcast on April 7, 1939, and ran through the summer. The mechanism of the quiz was just the thing for an old Sherlock Holmes buff like Perelman. A panel of fiction writers would be assembled to try to work out the plots of mystery tales from the clues and plot gimmicks sent in by listeners. Usually the conclusions reached by the literary experts diverged wildly from the progression the listeners had intended for their plots, but the program must at least have provided a bit of literary fun and some insider's shoptalk on which the whodunit fan could eavesdrop. Regular panelists included Frederic Dannay and Manfred Lee, the real-life personalities who fuse into the mystery-story composite the world knows as "Ellery Queen," and Perelman brought Dorothy Parker and Heywood Broun onto the airwaves in order to give the program some literate snap.

The next summer Perelman's sketches were among those of more than twenty writers and composers who supplied material for a revue designed to tour summer theaters called "Two Weeks with Pay"— sketches and songs more or less tied together by the theme of the great American vacation. Television has long ago put to death touring shows like this one, but the revue's pedigree is extremely impressive even if we might suspect that most of the material was either drawn from major productions already famous in their own right, or dusted off from those files of near-miss material every creative artist accumulates throughout his career. Rodgers and Hart, Cole Porter, Johnny Mercer, Johnny Green, and Ira Gershwin had their songs included, the dances were staged by Gene Kelly (there were more than thirty dancers and singers for the troupe), and Hiram Sherman headed the tour cast. Never formally reviewed by any of the major critics, *Two Weeks with Pay* must be presumed to be a one-shot affair that did not have quite enough success to either take on a life of its own or sire offspring.

Chapter Two
Perelman's Progress
Tragedy

The 1940s were to be very good to Perelman's career, but the decade began with a family tragedy: Nathanael West was killed on November 22, 1940, returning to Los Angeles from a hunting trip in Mexico. He had just purchased a matched pair of Purdy shotguns for $740 and had been anxious to try these nonpareil weapons on some quail. Eileen McKenney West, Nathanael's wife of eight months, was also killed in the two-car accident caused by her husband's negligence at the desolate Imperial Valley intersection of California routes 111 and 80 near El Centro. The day before, and unbeknown to West, his best Hollywood friend, Scott Fitzgerald, had died of heart seizure, and Perelman, who in April had been witness and best man at his brother-in-law's wedding, was now the escort for West's body as it was brought back to New York on the same Santa Fe Super Chief that was bearing Sheila Graham, Fitzgerald's mistress, back to the East after her tragedy. The only survivor in West's station wagon had been his hunting dog, Julie, and eventually the pointer bitch, terrified and badly slashed with splinters of automobile safety glass, was adopted by the Perelmans and brought to the Pennsylvania farm West and his sister and her husband had bought together in 1932.

A comic writer can do very little with such dark and terrible events, but Perelman never wrote about West's life and death in a more serious vein, either. Just as with his own parents, or with his children, or with Laura's death in 1970, Perelman's professional writing bears only traces of his deepest feelings and most sensitive concerns.

Verne and Todd

In the decades from 1940 to 1960, Perelman published no fewer than 171 short pieces—twelve books worth of comic prose. He has called them "sportive essays," for want of a better term and reports that the *New Yorker* labels them "casuals" (*M*, 431). But he claims the best way to describe his occupation would be to write on the dotted line the French term "feuilletoniste" (*M*, 431); writer of little leaves—that is, a master of miniatures. Since this noun is in no danger of becoming a household word in America, we will have to call him a writer of short comic essays and let it go at that.

In the 1950s Perelman was to interrupt the writing of his short comic essays in order to create a long motion picture script for Avrom Hirsch Goldbogen—"better known to the world of entertainment and various referees in bankruptcy as Michael Todd." The picture, famous in its own era but now as dated as a stereopticon slide, was *Around the World in Eighty Days*.

Gritting his teeth, Perelman would go so far as to concede Mike Todd's personal magnetism; in fact, there is an undeniable appeal that draws all of us to admire that producer's piratical recklessness and unexampled *chutzpah*. From the beginning, Todd had conceived of *Around the World in Eighty Days* as a sort of filmic assault on *The Guinness Book of World Records*: 46 major stars in cameo roles, 34 directors shooting in 112 locations, 140 full-scale sets and 74,685 costumed actors (15,612 of them with beards); 7,959 animals (including 512 rhesus monkeys), and with the whole business captured in the new 70 millimeter wide-angle process that Todd, who had nothing to do with its invention, modestly named after himself. Although all this press-agent quantification sounds especially ridiculous a quarter of a century after the event, at the time the picture was made sheer spangled magnitude was thought to be a virtue in itself. In fact, the fantastic expense and complexity of the enterprise was the movie's only real production value—for Todd had realized with his show-man's instinct that people would enjoy simply knowing that all that money had been sent off into the outer darkness; he was one of Barnum's disciples, and Barnum had discovered a century before Todd that people will usually pay good money to see good money spent. Conspicuous consumption is wonderful box office—at least until the novelty wears off.

It is also important to remember that until about the mid-1960s the production teams and their backers were still fighting desperately to win back their audience from television; and for a time during the 1950s sheer giantism was one of the industry's panaceas. And for a little while, giantism worked. *Giant, The Ten Commandments, War and Peace, The Greatest Show on Earth, Ben Hur,* and *Cleopatra* were some of the names Hollywood gave to its enormous, slow-witted offspring, and Todd was perhaps able to raise money for his supercolossal project precisely because the bankers who control the movie industry sensed that sheer grandiosity would turn the trick, and that Todd's brand of it might well bring in a winner. And so he did. He even got to marry Cleopatra as one portion of his reward. And then Todd was killed in a plane crash in 1958 instead of keeping a promise he had made during his epic struggle: "As soon as the excitement dies down, I'm going to have a nervous breakdown. I worked for it, I owe it to myself and nobody is going to deprive me of it."[1]

If Perelman was always to think Irving Thalberg overrated, his feelings for Mike Todd are an even headier mixture of loathing, fury, and contempt; but with this difference—there is amusement there— for at least Todd never bothered to impersonate an intellectual, and no one would ever recall Todd, as old Hollywood hands recalled Thalberg, sitting out in the hallway in Lee Francis's famous whorehouse reading *Variety* while this or that famous guest satisfied himself behind closed doors. Todd was as tough and macho as they come, and Perelman even suspects that he really was "made of the stuff they usually put on the points of fountain pens, iridium, the hardest metal known."[2] And if misery breeds copy, Todd created a good deal of both.

One summer morning in 1955 Todd phoned Perelman's agent and suggested that the writer meet with him at the Beverly Hills Hotel to discuss the terms of a draft filmscript for the Verne epic. Perelman never identified the genesis of that call, but perhaps one of Todd's advisers had noticed Perelman's punning familiarity with the novel from *Westward, Ha! or Around the World in Eighty Clichés*, or perhaps had even recommended Perelman to Todd from the content of the "Cloudland Revisited" piece, "Roll On, Thou Deep and Dark Scenario, Roll," which had appeared in the *New Yorker* for August 16, 1952. Strange are the ways of Hollywood, but strangest of all would be to imagine that someone like Todd had the slightest personal interest in an erudite stylist like Perelman.

In any event, producer and writer came to an agreement on terms—or at least Perelman did: he found that it was next to impossible even to collect either his salary or his royalties from the famous scofflaw ("slippery as a silverfish"), and, quoting his literary idol James Joyce, describes Todd as being always "as full of wind and piss as a barber's cat."

The plot of Verne's great novel is simplicity itself, and just the sort of simplicity the movies do best—all action and exteriors, with Phileas Fogg's effort to win a famous 1872 Reform Club bet over a whist table hurrying events along like a lighted fuse to create suspense: can he really girdle the globe in only eighty days? No one can fault Todd's casting: David Niven was the very essence of British *sangfroid* as Fogg, Robert Newton made an excellent archvillain as Inspector Fixx, and thirteen of the most photogenic countries of the world provided more exotic backdrops than a half-dozen issues of the *National Geographic*.

As the major writer for a project that was far from completely scripted even as filming began, Perelman accompanied the main unit to Spain for the bullfighting sequences, which are mostly slapstick sight-gags featuring Fogg's batman, Passepartout (played by the Mexican comedian Cantinflas). In accordance with Todd's intention to use a celebrity wherever he could insert one, the great bullfighter Luis Dominguín appears in that particular tomfoolery, but on the other side of the camera Perelman witnessed Todd's quarrel with one of his directors, John Farrow, which resulted in the first of what were to be many dismissals (in his assault on the *Guinness Book of World Records*, Todd did not neglect to try at the entry for Most Lawsuits, One Motion Picture Production).

The company next moved on to London to shoot the Reform Club interiors, Lloyd's underwriting offices, and Fogg's home in Burlington Gardens. Todd, who was of course wildly overextended with his finances, took up residence at the Dorchester Hotel in a suite that Perelman describes as being "of such barbaric tastelessness that it must have been shipped piecemeal from Las Vegas to make him feel at home."[3] Todd felt at home, all right. His natural home was at the center of the action, and if it took a lot of wherewithal to stay in the center, his attitude was that it was only money—and other people's money, at that. Caviar by the cubic meter, champagnes the vintages of which would have awed an Ian Fleming, one dollar Flor de Magnicico cigars, long-distance phone calls to his aerie in California—Todd never stopped living off the uppermost portions of the most succulent hog just because of some pedestrian reason like not having any money, and one can only admire his grasp of the realities of his finance: "I was a million in the hole. What was I supposed to do, cut down on my cigars?"[4]

One item he did cut down on did effect a real economy, though: salaries. Perelman speaks for almost everyone connected with the operation when he recalls that, "week after week, it took cajolery, pleas, and threats of legal action to collect one's salary."[5] Perelman, at least, finally hit upon an admirable solution. When Todd had lined up more stars for cameo appearances and needed to furnish them with lines to speak and business to perform, he tried again to inveigle prose out of Perelman in exchange for some Scheherezade-like visions of the future including "milk-white lovelies surpassing Jane Russell," as well as standard wish-fulfillment items like yachts and racehorses. Nothing doing. By this time Perelman realized there was only one way to deal with Todd, and so the two of them evolved a working relationship that would have made Irving Thalberg stare in disbelief: every night Perelman would meet Todd in a Beverly Hills parking lot, and, once he had Todd's payment in his left hand, turn over to the moviemaker a page of script with his right. This furtive exchange of paper for paper continued for weeks, and the two of them were perhaps lucky that they were not arrested by plainclothes narcotics agents on suspicion of engaging in the Hollywood cocaine trade. But if misery breeds copy, it also loves company, and Perelman was no doubt heartened to learn much later from David Niven that the actor had to wait until five months after the movie had opened—and it was an immediate and colossal hit—to receive his own stipend for his last week's work. And Niven had starred in the damn thing, not merely written it!

Perelman's craftsmanship with the scripting was remarked by several reviewers. In *Holiday*, Harry Kurnitz noted that even "if there is no discernible trace of the Master's lunatic genius in the dialogue and devices, it remains a creditable arrangement of the story to fit the attached extravaganza, with the plot and characters playing second, third and fourth fiddle."[6] The *Time* reviewer found Perelman's script a "deft, witty spoof of Verne's book, which in turn was a spoof of the English, so that the moviegoer often experiences the refined pleasure of laughing at a man who is laughing at somebody else."[7] The usually sniffy John McCarten of the *New Yorker*, a critic notoriously difficult to please, commented that "most of the time Mr. Perelman's inventions are diverting, whether he is showing us an irritable clubman complaining about the heavy footfalls of a cat in the reading room or having his balloon-borne travellers scoop snow off an Alp to chill a bottle of champagne."[8] McCarten did complain of the film's near-geological running time (2 hours and 55 minutes), but conceded that Todd's *chef d'oevre* was "a movie, all right, and, except for its length, a good one."

Todd was always to insist that only his expertise and instincts had made the movie a good one, and he claimed that even his chief writer had been ready to take off on a surrealistic tangent at the climax of the tale, when Fogg, who believes his bet to be lost, suddenly realizes that he has an extra day because of his crossing of the International Date Line and must race to the Reform Club in order to snatch victory from out of the clockwork of defeat. "I had to keep fighting so that the thing wouldn't get out of hand," Todd was quoted in *Newsweek* a good deal after the fact. "Instead of having Phileas Fogg walk into the club and win his bet at the end of the picture, S. J. Perelman wanted to have Santa Claus pop out of the fireplace, whisk off his whiskers, and turn out to be Groucho Marx."[9] The producer does not say whether or not Perelman offered him this bright idea in a Beverly Hills parking lot after a hard day at the typewriter, and one might reasonably assume that the writer's working conditions may have had a marked effect on his appreciation for the surreal by the time he spoke. At any rate, Fogg remained Niven, and won his gamble. Todd remained Todd, and won his, too.

Although Perelman deputized Hermione Gingold to receive the Academy Award for him, and though he used the statuette for years as a doorstopper in his Greenwich Village office, he would gruffly admit a certain amount of pride in his achievement: "I think everyone who receives an Oscar, even myself, is delighted."[10] But Perelman did not

move back to Hollywood to capitalize on his new credentials—once
again we must accuse him of artistic integrity. And for all practical
purposes, he was done with the movies.

And More Verne

But not with Verne. In 1970, on the pretext of ascertaining whether a
man could indeed girdle the globe in eighty days using transportation
more or less like that available to Fogg, Perelman performed the
journey he details in "Around the Bend in Eighty Days" (included in
Vinegar Puss). It was a trip "remarkably without incident,"[11] or at least
without misery, a condition no doubt due in large part to Perelman's
astute choice of a Passepartout to accompany him: a very large and
good-looking Southern belle from Pass Christian, Mississippi, he
calls "Sally-Lou Claypool": "six feet one, with a figure that fractured
the senses."[12] One of his interviewers claimed that, although Perelman would not discuss the tag, he had long had a "reputation as a
literary Lothario,"[13] a reputation the writer does not exactly scotch by
reporting that, as he left from the Reform Club with the spectacular
Sally-Lou in tow, "One lady, in tendering me a farewell gift box,
observed sweetly that it was an editorial comment on my companion."[14]

Once again, Perelman's perceptions along the route are marked by
literary disillusion. He always anticipates the exotic things he will
visit by previewing them through the rose-tinted spectacles of romantic literature of his youth, but of course reality, once he arrives at it,
can only be regarded through those colorless, commonsensical steel-
rimmed eyeglasses Perelman acquired in Paris during the expatriate
era. Life always takes away the Technicolor. Thus, a visit to the
Topkapi Museum in Istanbul is a side-trip into a book (from off the
main trip into a book), for Perelman really only wants to ascertain if
an acrobatic jewel thief could really steal a gem-encrusted dagger out
of the electromagnetic field of its burglar-alarm system, as set forth in
the Eric Ambler thriller from which the movie *Topkapi* was made. The
museum guards, sick of the question, tell him that Ambler's gimmick was the Turkish equivalent of "sheer flapdoodle." Nor is the
train from Istanbul to Erzurum the junior version of the Orient

Express that Perelman's travel agent had promised him, complete with veiled charmers scented with patchouli and monocled Mitteleuropean operatives puffing at those Sobranie cigarettes which Graham Greene and Ian Fleming assure us are the smoke of spies. It turned out to be "a slow train through Arkansas, bulging with country folk and their turbulent possessions." The mountains of Turkey were all poverty and soldiers, the weather was snowy and bleak, the cuisine was mostly goat cheese and "bread resembling Michigan peat moss." The Middle East smelled of "open drains openly arrived at," air-conditioned Manhattan delicatessens redolent of pastrami and dill pickle were half the world away, and the disease and poverty endemic in the Fertile Crescent are a sharp contradiction of the world implied in the *Rubáiyát*: it is all nothing more than "a Muslim version of Appalachia."[15]

Because Fogg did it, Perelman and his lovely companion (now twenty-three days into the journey) traveled across a few yards of India aboard an elephant named Rosebud—at least Sally-Lou did, for Perelman found the swaying and pitching of the animal's howdah the next best thing to being seasick. Worse torments soon presented themselves. A fellow passenger on a British steamer asked Perelman's opinion as a writer of who was better, Jacqueline Susann or Harold Robbins, and in Hong Kong the impact of piledrivers preparing Asia for its tallest new building was powerful enough to make the spoon dance in one's coffee cup, and of course signified to Perelman defilement of the East by commerce. Facing the final leg of the trip, a nineteen-day Pacific crossing accompanied by hundreds of quacking, blue-haired American women and their balding spouses—"practical jokers, self-made men, close friends of General MacArthur," as Perelman had characterized them in *Swiss Family Perelman*—the writer takes the literary advice of an old friend he meets in Hong Kong and flies back to the States in a 707, leaving Sally-Lou to fly back to London on her own and accept a marriage proposal from a Cal Tech discus-thrower.

Finally capitulating to the letter of the text, though, Perelman completed the last segment of his self-imposed global circuit on the *Queen Elizabeth II*—and endured on the Atlantic all those blue-haired and balding Philistines with their new clothes and bingo games that he had flown over the Pacific to avoid. "I felt I had paid my debt to Phileas Fogg," Perelman comments at the end of the voyage, which finally ended, by no coincidence, exactly eighty days after he had begun. After almost half a century of infatuation, Verne's most faithful fan had finally performed an act of tribute worthy of his idol.

Perelman on Stage: *One Touch of Venus* and *The Beauty Part*

Perelman said that it is not seeing his prose in print, and certainly not seeing his own name on a screenplay that provided him with his greatest thrills as a writer. Beyond all comparison, he claimed, it is the excitement of the theater that provides the "keenest distilled satisfaction a writer can get."[16] Nothing matches the nervous excitement of a first night, when the atmosphere combines Monte Carlo with delivery room: have you "given birth to a monster or an absolutely beautiful and profitable baby?" In October, 1943, after years of gestation, Perelman and his Broadway cohorts created out of words and music a beautiful and profitable baby. *One Touch of Venus* was a hit.

Many talented people were involved. Mary Martin[17] played a statue of Venus who comes to life and, in accordance with the laws that govern all statues coming back to life, falls in love with the character responsible for freeing her—in this case, an ordinary fellow Perelman identified in a letter to Groucho as "a small schnükel of a barber."[18] Kurt Weill, famous for the music in *The Threepenny Opera*, created the tunes—of them, "Speak Low" still enjoys a life of its own—and Ogden Nash wrote the lyrics as well as collaborated with Perelman on the book. The choreography was Agnes de Mille's, and the musical comedy was staged by Elia Kazan long before he became a director famous for employing the Stanislavsky metaphysics in *A Streetcar Named Desire*. Lewis Nichols of the *Times* was so deeply impressed by *One Touch of Venus* he called its arrival at the Imperial Theatre a "millenium,"[19] and Robert Garland of the *Journal-American* found the story "endearingly cockeyed," with a "Gilbert and Sullivan flavor to the libretto and lyrics." Veteran critics like Louis Kronenberger of *PM* found the musical "unhackneyed and imaginative," and John

Chapman of the *Daily News* noticed that Cole Porter was in the first-night audience "cocking an attentive ear." What could be sweeter to the creators of *One Touch of Venus* than to arouse the admiration and envy of America's greatest musical-stage genius? However, Perelman's contributions did not escape the sort of criticism and caveat his stage work has always elicited. Ward Morehouse of the *New York Sun* peevishly claimed that "lines that must have seemed enormously glib and funny in the script are surprisingly lifeless when spoken from the stage,"[20] and Kronenberger mentioned in passing that he sometimes found the dialogue fatiguing, its efforts at cleverness often "too strained, or at least too literary."

Even though the plot of *One Touch of Venus* is genetically derived from the ancestral ur-plot of all American musical comedies—boy meets girl and so on—a couple of its particulars are representative of Perelman's constant concerns.

Roughly summarized, the things that take place on the stage in front of us are a combination of *A Midsummer Night's Dream*, a Goldoni farce (all mistaken identity and marriage schemes), and a Dr. Fu Manchu thriller. The Shakespearean element is taken over from the short story from which the musical's book was derived, "The Tinted Venus," by a former *Punch* editor whose *nom de plume* was "F. Anstey" (Thomas A. Guthrie). Anstey had of course found it in *A Midsummer Night's Dream*: Titania, queen of the fairies, opens eyes anointed with a love-potion put there by Puck under orders from her leige lord, King Oberon; upon the most famous awakening in all comedy, she finds a "rude mechanical," Bottom, complete with an ass's head, in her field of vision. This, as they say, leads to complications. In the musical, the moment of awakening is again the moment of comic enslavement: "You are my lover," Venus tells the little *schnükel* of a barber when he playfully slips an engagement ring on her stone finger in order to prove to himself that his mortal fianceé has a finger whose perfection bears comparison with that of the goddess of love herself. And here, of course, is the plot: the young man is engaged to be engaged, and his countrymouse fianceé is due to arrive on the bus tomorrow in order to claim that ring. Anyone can see the comic possibilities, down to and including the producers of the "I Dream of Jeannie" television series, who were able to squeeze scores of twenty-six minute playlets out of the same semiplagiarized situation.

Just below the surface of the situation we find a couple of premises peculiar to the world of fantasy and musical comedy—premises that have little to do with real life but deserve attention precisely because they do not. The barber, Rodney Hatch (played by Kenny Baker in the 1943 production), desires only to be respectable, and we are never to doubt that he loves Gloria with every atom of his one-dimensional nature; every aspect of the comedy depends on those verities, which we are asked to assume for the duration of the play are as immutable as the behavior of iron filings in a magnetic field, even though the merest hint of common sense or common psychology would cause this aspect of the plot to disintegrate at the first touch.

At all costs, Rodney must keep fianceé Gloria from finding out about the other woman; he must also keep his landlady, Mrs. Moats, from evicting him for carrying on in his rooms with the other woman (this is, after all, 1943); and he must also contend with the machinations of the fussy, poisonous, charming, millionaire aesthete to whose museum he had been summoned for a professional shave in the first place—this is Whitelaw Savory, a part that would have been perfect for Rex Harrison, the archetypal Pygmalion—Higgins, or perhaps for Clifton Webb (John Boles played it in the original).

Whitelaw Savory is a far more interesting creation than the one-dimensional Rodney. At first we find the millionaire leading a brainless art-appreciation class toward the flippant rejection of the great painterly achievements of the past: "Kindly unlearn your Romneys and your Rembrandts,/Only the recent is worthy of your remembrance!"

But Venus freed from stone is a reincarnation of Savory's lost love from long ago, and suddenly delivered from his narrow and artificial aestheticism, he will do anything to capture her for himself (in other words, the plot has an embarrassment of love complications). He pursues Venus, Venus pursues Rodney. Savory's passion will stop at nothing, but the passions of a Cytherean brotherhood sworn to avenge the theft and profanation of their holy statue is even more deadly, and eventually Savory ends up in limbo.

The climax of *One Touch of Venus* is purest Perelman. Bewitched by magic into abandoning his sweetheart, Gloria—only the blackest magic could break *that* spell, of course—Rodney succumbs to the goddess's charms and agrees to marry her. But Venus's vision of the Staten Island bungalow and the frumpy lower-middle class future awaiting her—"After Dick Tracy, you'll come first," Rodney assures her—convinces her to return to the magic realm on the other side of the looking glass: the impossibility of a petty-burgher life of "Don Ameche double bills," Coca-Cola, and especially kids frightens her back to Olympus. Few other writers would have made an act of aesthetic revulsion the climax of a Broadway musical.

One Touch of Venus ran for 567 performances before going on tour and was sold to Universal-International Pictures for the then princely sum of $150,000. But as usual, Hollywood was able to effortlessly transform rainbows into a mud puddle, and the film was abominable. "A second-rate brand of slapstick has replaced the musical's gossamer style," Bosley Crowther wrote, and went on to call unchivalrous attention to change in casting: "The beauty and grace of Mary Martin are missed in Ava Gardner's lankier form."[21] For some reason only three of Weill's songs were retained, and one can be sure that Perelman's best quips—"all my teeth are wearing little sweaters," a character with a hangover says—were snipped out of the celluloid version.

Since their association had worked one miracle, Perelman and Ogden Nash naturally tried again, but this time with no success. Quite otherwise. The effort was called *Sweet Bye and Bye*, and "closed in Philadelphia like a ten-cent mousetrap" in the fall of 1946, leaving twenty-three investors some $300,000 lighter for their faith. The show was to take place in the future, and in a black parody of Lincoln Steffens's remarks after returning from Russia in the 1920s, Perelman states that after the thing bombed, they had seen the future and it did not work.

The Hit That Failed: *The Beauty Part*

In a book she calls *Broadway's Beautiful Losers*, Marilyn Stasio speaks of a sort of aesthetic freemasonry of New York theatergoers who are invisibly joined to their brethren by a single, powerful bond: they saw the original S. J. Perelman play *The Beauty Part*, circa 1963. In the mythology of the Great White Way, the story of *The Beauty Part* occupies a peculiar niche: it is the hit that failed. But just as with John Keats or Anne Boleyn, an early death has lent a paradoxical immortality. Stasio is verifiably correct in reporting that there is an "unofficial but loyal confraternity of people who saw *The Beauty Part*," and that they share with each other a common experience that lifts them above the rest of humanity, "like having been together at Krakatoa."[22] Although the play ran for only eighty-five performances, *The Beauty Part* was a *success d'estime* that became the rallying point for a cult, and exhibit A in the indictment intellectuals of the theater level against Broadway in what they perceive as the continuing crisis of the performing arts in America: the reconciliation of the high arts with mass taste. For Stasio, Perelman's play was a beautiful loser because it was essentially caviar to the general, one more casualty to the Broadway system—defined by her to be an "art form forced to function as an industry," and so, of course an art form sacrificed to an industry—and "one of the most mismanaged industries in the free-enterprise system,"[23] to boot.

There was also a good deal of simple bad luck.

Bert Lahr, the great comic, both inspired the creation, and starred in the original production, of *The Beauty Part*. And John Lahr, his theater-critic offspring, described the play from the other side of the footlights as a "hilarious spoof on cultural prostitution."[24] There is no need to suspect nepotism in John Lahr's adjective: the play is very funny, especially if you have the sort of taste that finds a Neil Simon comedy nothing more than chocolate-covered sawdust.

The Beauty Part was created as a six-role opportunity for a comical tour de force by the senior Lahr, who plays, to quote Perelman's own captions: "a millionaire philanderer, a Hollywood agent, a Cambodian émigré, a septuagenarian restaurant tycoon, a Los Angeles judge, and a female magazine oligarch." If it can be said to have a theme, or at least a dominant attitude, *The Beauty Part* might be described as being a satiric commando raid on middle-class and upper-middle-class artistic pretensions—on the cult of self-expression and "creativity." As a play, then, we have a series of sketches and skits, more or less in the manner of a television special; and a satire; which is to say, a lesson in how to behave. Richard Gilman was disappointed to find the play more cartoon than commando raid, more skit than lesson. It entertained more than it taught: *"The Beauty Part* is cartoon comedy, which means among other things that its satiric velocity is curtailed and its virtues of personal statement and unbeholden spirit are considerably weakened by professional high-jinks and a broadness of platform."[25] Gilman sees this deficiency of "personal statement" as a negative quality, and the cartoonlike atmosphere of the high-jinks as vaguely disreputable—fun, perhaps, but trivial fun. And yet as far as I am concerned, all fun is precious, and the special atmosphere of Perelman's work is always more than enough reason for its own existence. Is there really such a thing as mere entertainment? The question is perhaps not as simple as it looks, and one might do well to ask how much of a lesson is there to be learned from *The Beauty Part* anyway: people act like pretentious fools, and they are fond of showing off. Is this fresh news? It would be hard to name a single comedy in the last twenty-five centuries of Western culture that failed to include mockery of sham and pretension somewhere in its texture, or did not include in its implications a negative judgment on fakery.

Gilman makes a more significant charge than lack of serious intention against Perelman, though: he finds Perelman "a superior cartoonist, but not a dramatist and especially not a visual one."[26] Howard Taubman of the *New York Times* noticed the same problem—it is nothing less than Perelman's basic problem with all acted versions of his work—when he pointed out that "standing on its own, the Perelman muse would not transpose easily and smoothly from the printed page to the theater," but that Lahr's genius "helps to make it home there."[27] John Chapman of the *Daily News* was enthusiastic, and called both Perelman and Lahr "gifted madmen," and Walter Kerr, himself a first-rate stylist, offered an interesting insight into Perelman's comic procedure by noting that he "loves words and hates the way people use them,"[28] although he cautioned that Perelman was being "incorrigible to the point of monotony in [his] giddy flirtation with words." Kerr was enthusiastic though, and announced that the play was the real thing: "it's against integrity, and it's funny."

All of the critics seemed to appreciate the fact that they were watching a Broadway comedy more or less organized around the Candide principle: young Lance Weatherwax, a sober and admirable young innocent freshly inoculated with culture at Yale University, moves out into the milieu of the arts in order to find Truth, but of course finds only upper-middle-class fakers, culture-peddling phonies, and cynical con men. If it is not immediately apparent why and how this quest comes to involve a Cambodian houseboy who directs Civil War films, stealing a script from a safe, the arrest of the ingenue for conspiring to emerge out of a giant cherry pie in order to dance with a companion impersonating a gorilla, a fake Los Angeles swami who practices human sacrifice, a visit to a red-baiting paranoid millionaire hiding out in a hothouse perpetually kept at 118°F., the lady publisher of *Shroud* and *Spicy Mortician* magazines (whose publishing firm is called Charnel House), and naturally, a good deal more, one can merely shrug, murmur "that's Perelman," and hope for a revival—or, God willing, an intelligently handled film. Notwithstanding Perelman's near-mortal allergy to celluloid, the play could make a good movie, more or less along the lines of Stanley Kubrick's *Lolita*, brought to the screen in 1962. The world deserves it.

The Newspaper Strike

The world deserved *The Beauty Part* as a stage production in 1963, too, but a conspiracy of misfortunes brought it low. The reviews were excellent as they were written for the major metropolitan dailies and the provincial columns, but on December 8, 1962, two weeks before the opening of the play at the Music Box Theater, the International Typographical Union went on strike, and if one point of their settlement demands was not really the extinction of Perelman's play, it might as well have been. New Yorkers were without their 5.5 million copies of various and sundry newspapers for the duration of the 114-day strike, and the harassed local radio and television organizations, doing what they could to keep the public abreast of front-page things, devoted little air-time to recitations of theatrical reviews written by columnists from a rival medium.

Michael Ellis, who produced *The Beauty Part*, dreamed up some clever expedients for distributing the critical good news. He wangled permission from the Consolidated chain-laundering establishments to include in about 100,000 fragrant bundles of returned laundry fliers for the faltering stage production printed up with rave notices. Picking up rolls of developed film at Arrow Photo outlets, startled New Yorkers—again about 100,000 of them—discovered ads for Perelman's masterpiece included gratis. There was a skywriting attempt and sidewalk criers in Revolutionary War outfits carrying sandwich boards. But as the advertising crisis deepened for all forms of retailing in the city, it was hard to bring a witty, acerbic, erudite stage production centering on *Candide* to the forefront of the metropolitan consciousness. Fifty percent of any Broadway production's ticket sales depend on mail-order advertising, much of it conducted by means of newspaper, and this was obviously diminished. The production team threw more than $40,000 in advertising in out-of-town papers, but New York plays need New York audiences, and the life-support system was mortally damaged.

Ellis may have been correct when he looked at his own $84,000 debt and concluded that "there is something inherent in the idea of the immediate impact of the total reviews, within the first week of the opening of the show, that seems to have a major effect." This is the condition that Stasio has made the major accusation of her book: Broadway productions survive as commodities, not works of imagination, and when they are denied their advertising umbilicus, they die. Ironically, Perelman's play makes the same comment about the same phenomenon—and the Furies whose business is the punishment of truth-tellers hunted it down and destroyed it.

Caviar

But the New York newspaper strike was not quite the whole story behind the decline and fall of *The Beauty Part*. Perelman's verbal acrobatics and perhaps the fact that the kind of people he was satirically attacking are the same people who buy all those expensive tickets to see Broadway shows might have had something to do with the play's failure at the gate. As Michael Ellis pointed out, there was no newspaper strike in Philadelphia during the out-of-town tryout, and yet the piece did not take off there, either. "We got very, very good notices in Philadelphia, but we did *no business* . . . [in three weeks] we grossed just about $25,000 *total*—which must be the all-time low for a show that got good notices."[29] In fact, the show had lost $40,000 even before it got a chance to lose a great deal more in New York. David Doyle, an actor who played six of the minor parts in the piece—there were seventeen performers playing about forty-five parts—sensed that the audiences "were either with it from the very beginning—realizing that they were in for something saucy and sassy—or it just sailed right past them."[30] Bob Ullman, the show's publicist, said that the high quotient of literary wit and the play's relentless and triumphant cynicism would have made a real triumph very difficult under the best of circumstances: it was "caviar for the masses . . . they were laughing at Bert Lahr's clowning."[31]

Ellis also made a complex mistake in handling the rental of the theaters for the staging of the production, and there is some truth in Perelman's melancholy observation that "there was much misman-agement and inefficiency . . . everybody concerned with the show really mishandled it."[32]

Ellis had signed a contract for the show to be only a temporary tenant at the Music Box Theatre on 45th Street (the site of Perelman's first Broadway revue, *The Third Little Show*), but no advance tickets for another venue could be sold until that site was determined—and once it was in fact determined (the Plymouth Theatre, just across the street), the public had no information from the papers about the switch, $5,000 was spent out of an exhausted budget just to move, and the Plymouth itself had been promised to a production of Lillian Hellman's play, *My Mother, My Father, and Me*, due to open there only a few weeks after Ellis had desperately relocated *The Beauty Part* into it. Rather than move yet again with even that move perhaps into another interim booking (at that time Broadway still had more shows than stages on which to play them), the producers decided to close down. And so *The Beauty Part* folded on March 9, 1963.

Bert Lahr, who had told an interviewer from the *New Yorker* that "I quite honestly feel that it's the funniest show I've ever been in"[33] (and Lahr had been in show business since 1910) was bewildered and immensely cast down. He was also sixty-seven years old, and the wonderful combination of Perelman and Lahr would never have another opportunity at a stage victory. Perelman called Lahr "the last of the great comedians," and even when Lahr would tinker with his lines or alter his situations, the writer admitted that the comedian could many times improve on them: "by his own peronality Lahr was able to take this thing and really give it a tremendous dimension."[34] One cannot help but feel that one of Broadway's great comic collaborations had been thwarted by sheer misfortune.

Although Perelman was eventually able to make some sort of copy out of the misery, the failure of *The Beauty Part*, so undeserved and accidental, put him into deep professional wrath. Harvey Orkin, at that time Perelman's literary agent, provides an insight into Perelman's personal response to the hit that failed: "The reviews were raves, and we thought the show was a smash. All the talk between us and the producers was about what we should do with the show in the third year, and who should be in the cast in the road company when the show went on tour, and whether to take the profits in spread. Sid was really flying high, and he took a trip to Africa. When we closed the show two months later, I finally had to cable Sid in Africa. He wrote a *New Yorker* piece about that cable, and in it I think he referred to his agent as 'Toby Swindler,' "[35]

Perelman, in fact, calls his agent "Toby Swingler" in the piece, altering that one key consonant just enough to avoid a lawsuit even while he suggests some show-business chicanery. The cable "Toby Swingler" sent Perelman in the comic piece concludes with the line "Earnestly advise you lengthen visit Seychelles as understand breadfruit plenteous and aggravations minimal," and Perelman cannot decide if he should return to New York to oversee the last days on earth his creation would enjoy. In the *New Yorker* piece, Perelman consults an African stargazer to see whether his return would be efficacious, and the sage declares from a handwriting sample that Swingler is "a trickster, a double-dealer,"[36] the sort of judgment which makes the implications of a literary mini-revenge on Perelman's part impossible to ignore. As Stasio observes, Perelman is "not always as just as he is funny,"[37] and that no one should ever confuse the writer's temperament with that of St. Francis of Assisi. This is the famous prickliness that Arthur Mizener saw both within and between the lines of Perelman's responses to the interviewers from the *Paris Review* when he spoke of "S. J. Perelman's comic awareness of his own thorny, self-doubting belligerence."[38] We must always remember that the comic creates his comedy by distilling vinegar back into champagne—that the usual processes of fermentation are reversed in that strange chemical reaction that creates first-rate comic writing.

Perelman Against the Grain

J. A. Ward pointed out that Perelman usually "introduces to the show business setting not a group of irreverent and destructive eccentrics [like the Marx brothers], but a naive worshipper of the fraudulent scene. Usually harmless, the Perelman protagonist craves success, but in his gullibility is invariably defeated by the conscience-less frauds who rule whatever papier-mâché empire it is that he seeks to invade."[39] Lance Weatherwax, the Candide-figure in *The Beauty Part* who wants to go beyond "mere money," is somewhat more innocent than is the usual Perelman alter ego, but if he was freshly laundered as he left the immaculate precincts of Yale, by the time he has journeyed through a half-dozen dens of iniquity he has taken on the smudges and stains of the milieu around him. At the climax of the play his father (Lahr in his incarnation as the millionaire garbage-disposal king, Milo Leotard Allardyce DuPlessis Weatherwax) creates a "mighty-tax-free foundation" for his son to control, the sole function of which will be to bring culture "into every American home." And so if Lance can cry out, "Me—the final arbiter of truth and beauty!" with some justice, he is still extending his own ego on his own terms (implicitly to the disadvantage of all other egos), and we have seen that his taste in the arts runs to film scenarios created out of cafeteria placemats singing hymns to the chocolate soda.

The elder Weatherwax also has the final comment on American culture as the curtain comes down: the kid loves Truth and Beauty, does he? Well, all the Truth and Beauty is microcosmically brought out on stage in a baby bassinet, and it turns out to be nothing more or less than fistfuls of cold, hard, cash, which Weatherwax and his wife proceed to fling about like celebrants at the Lindbergh parade. If

Perelman made the climax of *One Touch of Venus* an act of aesthetic revulsion against lower-middle-class banality, here at the climax of *The Beauty Part* we see that the affluent classes who control the arts have raised an impregnable fortress: a temple to the Muse of Mammon. It hardly needs to be pointed out that such cynicism is not the usual life-affirming message one bears away from a Broadway comedy, and John Lahr, who loved the play, realized full well that "Broadway was perhaps the wrong location to launch a debate about democracy and culture."[40]

Notice in passing the weightiness of those terms: democracy and culture. Although the delightful flapdoodle that Perelman has created would seem to be a temporary escape from such important concerns, *The Beauty Part* is in fact authentically subversive, even discomfiting, if we take the trouble to speculate about its implications.

At first glance, one cannot see much that is controversial in Perelman's comment that in his play he was lampooning "the frightening notion that everybody has to be creative; the barber has to paint pictures, the housewife has to take ballet lessons . . . I'm not really attacking anything. I'm all for them as long as they remain amateurs. But the amateurs are taking themselves seriously. They're trying to sell their stuff. They actually consider themselves artists. That, in the language of our time, bugs me."[41]

The notion is not quite polite, perhaps even a touch elitist, but the humanities establishment—the universities, the professional thinkers, the publishing concerns, the foundations and journals, almost everyone that uses the written word to make a living—has never faced up to the problems of *taste* in a mass democracy. And Perelman is really bothered about taste, which always must require at its core a sense of self-restraint, self-imposed limitations, an acceptance of "place," of fitness and decorum. And although it may smack of a dainty parlour cynicism, one might even argue that self-restraint—and so, necessarily, taste—is the most difficult of all virtues for a democracy to achieve. But here I hasten to add that there are other virtues which are immeasurably more important than self-restraint and taste—freedom of expression, freedom of career, freedom from the past, freedom of social mobility—which only a democracy can encourage.

In any event, the conflict between taste and the intense demands for self-realization that an open society encourages and rewards is a real one, probably an inherent condition of democracy. Class-bound societies automatically subdue that alarming sense of self-importance; after all, that is what social classes are for, and explains the real reason for its subtle police procedures like right forks and wrong accents. Anyone who has ever taught a creative writing class in an American university soon comes to realize that, although they will accept no criteria to objectively sustain their claim, most of the "amateurs" who enroll in such courses expect their efforts to be taken seriously and conceive that as Americans they have the right to regard themselves as serious artists. The condition that "bugs" Perelman may well be unavoidable. But one must also add that his satire may in part be generated by the nervous jealousy of a professional half a century in the business who does not like to see the vulgar swarm fooling around out there on the turf it has taken him most of his career to stake out. Perelman might have revealed an immodest glimpse of that vanity that spurs on every artist when he reveals that the genesis of *The Beauty Part* was a casual comment made by the elevator operator in his apartment building to the effect that he, the elevator operator, was "having trouble with" his second act. Reduced to its essence, Perelman's play is an effort to get everyone back in his proper place, and America has not yet been in a mood to heed that imperious command.

Page and Stage

The Beauty Part was in large part created out of the same material Perelman had been satirizing throughout his professional career, and in several instances it was lifted straight out of his own magazine pieces. In fact, the use of printed prose for speaking purposes created some of the difficulties theatergoers had with the play and perhaps contributed to its failure. Nabokov once wrote that our language needed a single word which would be defined as "To abridge, expand, or otherwise alter or cause to be altered, for the sake of belated improvement, one's own writings in translation."[42] In like manner, a term also cries out to be created as a single, efficient verb for expressing an author's use of his own material in a second reincarnation, and it would be especially useful in talking about *The Beauty Part*, where Perelman borrows heavily from Perelman. Auto-plagiarization? Self-recycling? Whoever comes up with a dictionary definition could illustrate it by pointing to the material Perelman resurrected from his own files for use in the play.

One of Bert Lahr's favorite roles in *The Beauty Part* was that of Harry Hubris, the Hollywood superagent Perelman modeled on the likes of Swifty Lazar or Myron Selznick—the character has the *chutzpah* peculiar to movieland nabobs: the smarmy unction of a head counsellor on parent's day at Camp Sunrise combined with the maddening and enviable gift of remaining invulnerable to insults and disapproval under any and all circumstances, especially ones which would humiliate the rest of us for the rest of our lives. Perelman has described the voice emanating from this sort of gargoyle as "full of gravel and Hollywood subjunctives . . . a flexible instrument that could shift from adulation to abuse in a syllable."[43] In the mind's eye and ear, then, one might combine the personae of Alan King, Barbra Streisand, Tony Ulasciwicz (the Watergate money-laundryman), Roy Cohn, and Portnoy's mother and come up with a fair approximation. But just as with Mike Todd, there is at least an atom or two of something perversely endearing about the character, too, perhaps just a touch of self-parody, that mitigates the worst of our exasperation.

Harry Hubris first appeared as a Hollywood producer in a piece Perelman called "Portrait of the Artist as a Young Mime" before he transposed it almost directly into the texture of *The Beauty Part*. The character is the same on stage as on page, right down to the $1,200 saffron polo coat (obligatory Hollywood mufti for plausible highbinders, evidently), and the wonderful combination of Yiddish inflection and show-biz Americanese that characterizes his discourse: "Remember this lug don't know from beauty or the Muse,"[44] he tells Perelman's mouthpiece Zuckmeyer in "Portrait," attempting to get Zuckmeyer, a painter, to coach a young actor in the correct mannerisms of his profession.

Another of Lahr's parts, that of the lady publisher Hyacinth

Beddoes Laffoon, one of Perelman's most wonderful names, appeared in the *New Yorker* in a playlet called "The Hand That Cradles the Rock," and at least two more of the Broadway production's key situations were derived from pieces[45] written first as prose "casuals" long before they were transferred to the stage. The fact that these pieces were themselves inspired into nutty life by "straight" news articles Perelman had glimpsed in the course of his prodigious reading perhaps begins to explain the overly literary quality criticized by many of the people who worked with the play or reviewed it professionally. As Michael Ellis gently phrased the problem—and it is a real problem—"Sid is a verbal writer, and *The Beauty Part* is a special play for special people."

It is possibly no accident that the most popular scene in the play, and the interlude that Bert Lahr singled out for the *New Yorker* as his favorite, was written hastily in an effort to prop up the sagging second act and was as much a product of Lahr's gift for improvisational genius as it was of Perelman's pen. This is the "Smedley scene," act 2, scene 3, about a character that might even owe something to real millionaire paranoids like Howard Hughes.

Smedley is the Birchite owner of the Smedley Snacketeria chain, and, in an effort to protect himself from creeping pinko infiltration and violence to his person delivered by means of deadly bacilli, he stays perpetually ensconced in his glassed-in hothouse, swathed in mufflers, woolens, and laprobes, and waited upon by strong-arm henchmen. Perelman reminded Marilyn Stasio that he has been a longtime admirer of Raymond Chandler, the original purveyor of sinister southern California right-wing eccentricity, and that Smedley had been wafted into his imagination more or less directly from the pages of that great creator of the American *policer*: "On two occasions in his detective novels," Perelman said of Chandler, "he had scenes laid in a hothouse, once with a rich old lady in Pasadena."[46] By relaxing his efforts just a little and allowing Lahr to wing it more than usual, Perelman helped the scene become the most memorable and hilarious in the entire play. After all, the play was in Philadelphia at the tryout at the moment, time was short and hysteria high, and Perelman had to swallow his pride.

Up to that point in the development of the play he had no doubt been much too fretful about whether or not the actors were delivering precisely what he had worked so diligently to get just right on the page. Most writers are word-proud, and Perelman was doubtless as stubborn as any. Director Noel Willman had suffered from Perelman's perfectionism during rehearsals and worried that it might begin to inhibit Lahr, who, like all great comedians, was a perfectionist in getting the material in just the right shape for himself: "Often, to Perelman's rage [Lahr] would suddenly take lines and change them. Perelman hated Lahr to change a line or to substitute one of his own, or slightly change it, or anything like that. He *hated* that."[47] But in the Smedley scene Lahr was given free rein largely because time was short and Perelman had no long-standing literary investment in the interlude, and so the performance became the centerpiece of a remarkable comedy and perhaps the closest to George S. Kaufman's brand of comedy that Perelman was ever to come: political playfulness and candy-coated satire.

It is interesting to learn that when the Smedley scene was penciled in, Lahr, a Jewish comedian speaking a Jewish writer's lines, was at first concerned that the political backlash might remove the bit from its cartoonlike comic empyrean—after all, aren't those who mock red-baiting actually encouraging reds? But when the laughs boomed back across the footlights, this particular sequence became one of Lahr's most famous performances, and Perelman became most consummately a playwright instead of a prose stylist recycling his pieces for the stage, finally realizing that his spoken jokes were not going to get the second chance the reading eye affords them. Perelman himself later told *Newsweek* that "a playwright is like a tailor. He has to fit the pants to a man who will stand in front of a triple mirror"[48]—that it is the actor who must make the lines work out there in front of the audience. The image Perelman chooses here is ingenuously humble: not a painter or an architect, but a tailor. One cannot help feeling that he learned a great deal from the experience and that under happier circumstances the play might have initiated a fine comic partnership between word-tailor and stage-clown. "From my point of view, it was an ideal collaboration," Perelman said of working with Lahr, an observation poignantly edged in funereal black crepe after the failure of the fates to provide another opportunity for this collaboration to continue.

Harvey Orkin felt that the Perelman—Lahr collaboration was potentially the great collaboration of contemporary Broadway comedy, but that it was somehow Perelman's special affliction to always be in the wrong place when Jove dropped a thunderbolt. Perhaps his nature even attracted thunderbolts. "He's like that character out of Al Capp, Joe Bltsfks," Orkin said of his ex-client, after Perelman had already limned him as "Toby Swingler." "Whenever he's around you know something's gonna happen. It's like having a picnic: you have this right and that right and everything's all set; you got the sandwiches, you got the martinis—but you forgot the gas."[49]

Or you forgot to warn yourself that the newspapers were going to go out on strike for 114 days.

Chapter Three
Autumn and Winter
Playful Poison

During the 1960s Perelman published two collections—*The Rising Gorge* and *Chicken Inspector No. 23*—and during the 1970s three more—*Baby, It's Cold Inside, Vinegar Puss*, and, in 1977, at the age of seventy-three, *Eastward Ha!* His productivity was undiminished and once again we have to accuse Perelman of artistic and personal integrity: he did not mellow with time and usage, *á la* a vintage wine or meerschaum pipe; he did not start pandering to younger writers with gracious septuagenarian reviews in the *Sunday Times*; he did not take part in the annual Bread Loaf Writers' Conference; and he especially did not settle down as a lovable mossbacked elder statesman of comic prose in an Ivy League English department—and every English Lit department in the Ivy League would be happy to have had him grace its catalogs.

Neither the celluloid mills of Hollywood nor the diploma mills of the heavy industry J. D. Salinger called "America's United English Department" could ever successfully seduce him into their respective harems—at least not to stay. "My sole ambition is to write as well as I can in the form of the short comic essay," he told Roy Newquist. "I want to go on improving the form if I can—which amounts to a rather modest ambition."[1]

Laura West Perelman died in April, 1970, a personal loss her widower spoke of nowhere in his published writing. Perhaps the severity of his loss was reflected, however, in the fact that by the October of that year he had relocated himself to London, announcing that his emigration would be once and for all. We might even be presumptuous enough to surmise that the angry dismay he exhibited toward Manhattan and the then-repugnant political atmosphere in the United States was perhaps one means that he had contrived of dealing with his grief: but one can only speculate posthumously about the feelings of a most private public man, and his annoyance with such efforts to psychologize him with clumsy questions or probe his most sensitive concerns with blunt inquiry has long since become an item of common knowledge in the literary subculture.

"You have only to go to England, for example, to see a country that still nourishes and appreciates her eccentrics," Perelman once told Roy Newquist, obviously implying that he included himself among the eccentrics. "This isn't true here. We're not interested in the eccentric or the old person." Nor was he fond of air pollution in New York City (not a very popular phenomenon to anyone whose opinion is on record, as far as I know): "Plants can live on carbon dioxide, but I can't. I think T. S. Eliot used the phrase 'twice-breathed air.' I'd hesitate to say how many times the air in New York has been rebreathed."[3] It is also important to recall how in 1970 the United States was still prosecuting its children's crusade in Vietnam under the leadership of Richard Nixon, and these facts struck Perelman as utterly repulsive; he found himself in a land beset with "jingoism" and "political fatuousness," perhaps hastening toward thermonuclear apocalypse through the stupidity of our political leadership—"whizzes like Richard M. Nixon will get us [to extermination] pretty fast," Perelman sighed. All you had to do was give them a little time. The only advice he had for the rest of us was "Duck—for the night is coming." Besides, English reviewers had always been more than kind to him, and the reputation that would proceed him in literary London would be very pleasant to live with over there. He was more of a celebrity in style-conscious England than he would ever be in his native land. Important literary voices in the British press "put me somewhere between P. B. Shelley and Andrew Marvell," he said, and this "Rhode Island kid twists his toe awkwardly in the hot sand"[4] in delighted embarrassment. And so, accompanied by headlines like "'Appalled' Perelman Going Eastward Ha!" the writer set off for merry old England to bask in celebrity during his golden years.

It did not work. Perelman was back in New York City by 1972. If he was not quite glad to be back in "the dirt, the disorder, the violence" of the New World metropolis or ready to pretend that we as a nation shouldn't be "bathed in shame about Vietnam,"[5] he had at the very least discovered that it was a mistake for a writer to try to permanently leave his origins. Perelman knew George Orwell's work thoroughly, and he might have found for himself this statement by the great British realist before he left his roots behind and had to sheepishly come back to reclaim them. Here Orwell is an Englishman speaking to Englishmen, but of course his statements are meant to describe a sort of universal law of nationalism: "above all, it is *your* civilization, it is *you*. However much you hate it, or laugh at it, you will never be happy away from it for any length of time . . . this side of the grave you will never get away from the marks that it has given you."[6]

England, Perelman admitted, had "too much gentility, civility, couth,"[7] and he sounded rather like an oyster pining for a grain of sand when he said that over there he had not found enough "at which to get irritated." He claimed that he missed "the tension, the give and take" of New York, the sheer gross vitality of the place. It was perhaps also a surprise to Perelman to discover that in England he had felt "out of touch with the idiom,"[8] obviously no minor torment for anyone who lives by writing parodic fiction. Alan Brien had guessed that even as Perelman had left for England the writer was on a real voyage to an imaginary destination, for the "tolerant, leisurely, graceful"[9] British Isles Perelman expected to find had long since vanished. And after he returned to America Perelman told Brien an anecdote that emphasized the fact that, as a man who still vividly recalled himself as the Jewish kid at Brown no one wanted in their fraternity, he did not like the snobbishness and rigidity of the English class structure: "I was talking in the street with a friend of mine, a real Cockney with a real Cockney accent. An upper-class Englishman I knew chanced by and I introduced them. I could see him looking at me and my friend. He didn't say anything, of course. But I could see him altering his attitude toward me and wondering why I was mixing with people of that sort. I couldn't stand that. A barrier rang down. That could have helped me decide to leave."[10]

The Bucks County farm with its memories was sold by now—"too much rural spendor,"[11] was Perelman's all-purpose explanation—and his only connection with the rural Delaware Valley was the barn down there where he still kept an "elderly, very cute" black 1949 MG YY

Tourer with red leather upholstery, bought about thirty years before in Bangkok, of all places. As another one of his misery-breeds-copy traveling stunts, Perelman evidently had plans to write up the results of his private recreation of the famous 1907 Peking-to-Paris auto race (in reverse: he started out from Europe). Brien described Perelman's Passepartout for this effort as a "formidable blonde named Delta Willis, who used to be in the business of organizing expeditions."[12] But Perelman evidently never wrote his account of the journey. Maybe the trip was simply too much fun, produced too few grains of sand around which to spin nacreous accounts of beautifully written disillusion.

Nor did *The Hindsight Saga*, the memoirs Perelman kept threatening us with, ever appear in book form, although a few fragments appeared in the posthumous collection *The Last Laugh* (1981).

The reasons why Perelman's memoir never appeared in his lifetime are perhaps not difficult to guess. Of all literary forms, the memoir is beyond all comparison the most intimate (setting aside the question of private letters we must assume were never intended for publication). Biographical reality is always at least partly a revealing account of one's own confusion and embarrassment and Perelman's use of it had always been highly stylized, his revelations purposely selected solely for their value as caricature and cartoon. And yet, to be interesting, to be worthwhile writing, a memoir must be intimate; but to write with intimacy about one's private life and the full range of one's feelings is probably the sort of step that Perelman would be extremely reluctant to take. And so Perelman the vulnerable human being inhibited Perelman the writer, and *The Hindsight Saga* seems to have remained only a series of mild little fragments about Nathanael West, Dorothy Parker, the Marx Brothers and writing for the movies. Perelman censored Perelman, right up to the end.

Television

By 1975, when Perelman was seventy-one and had just published *Vinegar Puss* (he has stated that the title was suggested to him by his own publicity photo), his reviews were already beginning to sound valedictory, perhaps even a touch elegiac. Nevertheless, several valuable insights are given to us by those reviewers. In the *New Republic*, Felicia Lamport spoke of the master as being already "enshrined alongside such golden 20's fellow-alchemists as Benchley" and Ring Lardner, and she also made the excellent point that he seemed "to have recognized his last from his first, and stuck to it."[13]

It is a great source of strength for any writer to recognize both early and late what he can do well. It is also surprisingly rare. Unlike Nathanael West, who could cynically turn out superior hackwork on demand precisely because he had no respect for it, Fitzgerald worked at being a screenwriter with a naive faith that he could make himself into a master of it—and of course failed utterly in the attempt. Setting aside successful departures like the 1963 play *The Beauty Part* (and as we have seen, even that play is heavily in debt to his prose), Perelman's work exhibited an astonishing consistency for fifty years. Each piece is about five or six pages long—ten would be exceptional. The gimmick of starting out with a bit of someone else's prose, the comic playlets, the Madison Avenue and Hollywood gargoyles in the cast of dramatis personae appear again and again. The vocabulary had looked like something out of a double-acrostic dictionary all along, and E. B. White, as a professional admiring a professional, is perfectly correct in singling out the beginnings of those pieces as absolutely unique—soaked with verbal and comic nitroglycerine, and as distinctive as a signature: "His pieces usually had a lead sentence, or a lead paragraph, that was as hair-raising as the first big dip on a roller coaster: it got you in the stomach."[14]

If Perelman was ashamed of himself for putting aside this unique prose of his own to work on movies just to "replenish the larder," his Hollywood efforts at least culminated with an Academy Award and the New York Film Critics citation. However, when he stooped to write for television, he failed to earn enough money to compensate him for the shame and his scripts were so heavily edited and revised that he could hardly bring himself to acknowledge his own contribution to the farrago. For a writer to whom style was just a little less important than oxygen, television must have been sheer Dante.

Perelman recapitulated his dismal television-writing career in a piece in his 1966 collection, *Chicken Inspector No. 23*, called "Be a Television Writer! Earn No Money!" (the title itself a parody of the claims made by those correspondence schools that advertise on match-books). In 1957 and 1958, Perelman was a staff writer for NBC's "Omnibus" series, a largely insipid effort to bring highbrow wit and culture, "living ideas" as they had it, to the American masses via the small screen. Perelman's "The Big Wheel," a salute to burlesque, at least allowed him to work with Bert Lahr, and like his co-scripting days with Ogden Nash, turned up a silver lining later.

But the saddest story of all is that of the CBS spectacular "Aladdin," Perelman's one collaboration with Cole Porter. Perelman dismisses the piece with a casual wisecrack, remarking that the day following the telecast, February 22, 1958, repairmen all over America found countless sets clogged with a kapoklike substance, "which, on analysis, proved to be 'Aladdin.'" As Brendan Gill summarizes it, the $500,000 musical fantasy was "roundly deplored by the critics,"[15] but the tragedy and misadventure that surrounded the presentation hardly stopped with its failure to please the viewers. The music was the last and perhaps the weakest that Cole Porter was ever to write before his death in 1964.

Porter, certainly one of the greatest songwriting talents in the history of the American musical stage, was sixty-seven at the time, and for the last twenty-one years of his life he had been suffering from injuries received during a horse-riding accident in which he had had both legs badly crushed. Intensely proud, immensely wealthy, but still smarting with the sting of the widespread critical disappointment with his previous two musical comedy scores (*Can-Can* in 1953 and *Silk Stockings* in 1955), Porter was talked out of semiretirement to try one more time by his agent, Irving "Swifty" Lazar—not coincidentally one of Perelman's models for the grotesque Hollywood producer he calls "Harry Hubris" in *The Beauty Part*. One of his biographers reports that Porter was deeply worried about protecting from further deterioration the "little reputation I still have left,"[16] but Lazar, who of course made his ten percent from the writer's royalties only if his writers were themselves getting paid, assured him that S. J. Perelman would be able to come up with a book worthy of grownups for the thing—this was going to be television with real class, not just something for the "six-year old mentality." We can also be fairly sure that Porter was subtly reminded that television was the only realm his genius had left unconquered. And so the old, crippled monarch set to work; and only one of his painkilling drugs was alcohol.

Porter ground out eight new songs and some theme music for the show, which was set in a sort of fairy-tale China, and there is a horrifyingly apt pathos in the anecdote George Eells tells of one isolated moment in the songwriter's agony that captures the terror of aging genius and the crass smarm of the media merchants with a single flashbulb pop. Cole called up Richard Lewine, the CBS executive in charge of the production for DuPont's "Show of the Month," and asked him if it was going to be all right to rhyme "gladden," "sadden," and "madden," with "Aladdin"—the creator of *Kiss Me, Kate*, was obviously groping for help amid the intense physical agony of his injuries and his disintegrating artistic self-confidence. Lewine, with payrolls to meet and sponsors to appease, replied thus to Porter's query: "Mr. Porter, you may even rhyme it with Bernarr McFadden—as long as we get the lyrics on time."[17]

Porter got them to the DuPont production team on time, but Jack Gould of the *New York Times* was to summarize critical reaction to the whole fiasco by offering yet one more rhyme to the songwriter: "To paraphrase one of Mr. Porter's less enticing lyrics, '*Aladdin* was saddin.'"[18] Nor was Perelman spared a session in the pillory: "It was hard to believe Mr. Perelman had a hand in last night's drab affair," Gould said, making a face like the duchess of Wonderland and calling the telecast "routined and labored," "keenly disappointing," "uninspired," and so on. He reserved special scorn for the casting of Sal Mineo, at the time still something of a teen idol in the afterglow of his success as the pathetic young psychopath Plato in *Rebel Without a Cause*, in the title role, for the young actor was both helpless and hopeless. Anna Maria Alberghetti was at least very pretty as Aladdin's vis-à-vis, and the producers had tried to provide some authentic supporting talent by hiring Cyril Ritchard to play a villainous magician and getting Basil Rathbone to walk through a smaller part merely to get his prestigious name into the credits.

Porter did not even watch the show, for at the time he was confined once more at Columbia-Presbyterian Hospital where he was operated on for an ulcer; and then in April, after a long and gallant struggle to avoid it, Porter finally consented to the amputation of his right leg.

His physicians had long feared that the bone ulcerations and osteomy-leitis that festered in the leg might spread into the rest of his system with mortal consequences, and the state of the limb—Porter had endured more than thirty operations on each of his legs—was finally deemed an immediate threat to his life. Porter's career ended at that moment, and one is left wondering what he and Perelman might have accomplished together if they had been collaborators for a stage musical while the songwriter was at the height of his powers. Certainly the pairing of America's wittiest and most cosmopolitan writer with our nonpareil Broadway songwriting talent could hardly have failed to create something memorable. Of the many near misses the fates arranged in Perelman's career (the failure of the 1962–63 play *The Beauty Part* being the most obvious, as we have seen), I feel that the collaboration that never was between Perelman and Porter may well represent the most poignant loss.

"The Changing Ways of Love" was the premier show of the CBS series "The Seven Lively Arts," yet another effort to make middle-high culture take root in the video wasteland. Perelman himself appeared in this effort, but it was still not a success. John Crosby, the television columnist, hosted the live presentation but forgot his contact lenses and could not read his commentary on the Teleprompter, and Jack Gould found Perelman in his tuxedo about as photogenic "as a pail of lard." At least that is what Perelman the misery-addict has him saying. Actually, Gould pointed out to his readership that "the Perelman sting and substance were sublime."[19]

So far, so bad. Or at least that is Perelman's modest pretense. "But," he goes on to say, "there appears to be a strange twisted logic in television, whereby an unbroken succession of failures often catapults a man to the top."[20] Shortly after the "Lively Arts" program, he parlayed a cold hand into what one would assume to be a choice assignment: writing a travelogue on London to be narrated by the famous Anglophile and London expert, Elizabeth Taylor, who had emigrated to America and world fame from Hampstead Heath in 1939.

Perelman had last seen that celebrated beauty in the possession of Mike Todd, one of the producer's choicest trophies from his siege and sack of the Hollywood stronghold. The writer recalled her "lying on a couch like Mme. Récamier" reading Cornell Woolrich's *The Bride Wore Black*, a cultivated allusion to Jacques Louis David's famous portrait of the eighteenth-century French salon-keeper (although the original omits the Woolrich paperback). Perelman had claimed at the time that Taylor seemed to know only three words, "Van Cleef & Arpels" (which gives her no credit for knowing an ampersand), but Taylor may well have remembered Perelman's work for Todd, and, two husbands later, Mrs. Richard Burton might have asked for Perelman's talents to grace her effort. In any event, Perelman was appointed to dream up something for her to say.

After a month's work on the script, Perelman got back together with the production team and the advertising representatives to put the sixty-minute piece into final shape for the filming; it was then that he discovered that in the realm of television the verb "to polish" indicates a ritual in which every interested party with money riding on a script gets to have a go at it, and "anything that might be construed as amusing is painstakingly removed." And once again it proved difficult for Perelman to collect his fee, evidently part of the routine of doing business with the media merchants. After all that, or perhaps because of it, Perelman reports that he could not bring himself to watch the final product on his own set when it was shown on Sunday, October 6, 1963.

A wise decision. Taylor, then at the height (or depth) of her notoriety as a love-thief, had been paid $500,000 by the Chemstrand Corporation to appear on camera at about twenty different London locations, each time wearing a different little something from Yves St. Laurent (one critic called the business "pin-up television"). The Tower bridge, Buckingham Palace, the Limehouse docks, the site of the "Wooden O" of the Globe Theater, a pub where young actors hung out, and so on, all captioned with good British lines out of Barlett's *Familiar Quotations* and interrupted every few stanzas for another commercial.

Grace Kelly had shown off her fief of Monaco and Jackie Kennedy had conducted us through the White House via video, so one of Taylor's friends may have been correct when she opined that the movie temptress had accepted the television offer in an effort to recover a little bit of the dignity she had lost during the Richard and

Sybil Burton *success de scandale*. Perelman shared the screen credits with someone named Lou Solomon, and his contribution was evidently mostly to assemble with scissors and paste a rather arty soundtrack composed of snippets from Elizabeth Barrett Browning, Conan Doyle, the younger Pitt, Wordsworth, Keats (Taylor throatily quoted a little "Endymion" to some ducks paddling about in the Serpentine, but they did not seem to mind), Winston Churchill, entries from Queen Victoria's diary on the death of Albert, and the like. "London is a city of words, and Elizabeth will *deal* in words," one of the show's producers had carefully explained. But Perelman, whose business has always been words, had little opportunity to make use of his own.

A casual image Perelman gave of himself during an interlude when he was writing a film script in Rome (and he would not even identify the picture that was made from it) summarizes in a single vignette his attitude toward all of his departures from his best efforts in prose. He reported that for this movie assignment he worked from eleven in the morning until just past one in the midday, dictating his script to a secretary who was a least theoretically bilingual. For lunch he always walked from his hotel over to Babington's, the famous English-style tearoom at the foot of the Spanish Steps, a locale a literary person almost reflexively associates with Keats's last days on earth (the poet died there in the company of Joseph Severn on February 23, 1821). But Perelman does not evoke so great a ghost as Keats's to brood over his betrayal of the muse. He just claims that he always passed "Gogol's commemorative table in the Via Sistina" with "eyes averted because I felt he was reproaching me for desecrating our profession."[21] The fact that Perelman really did feel a responsibility toward the achievements of the mighty dead, and so a sense of self-reproach for not trying to equal them, is one more indication of his integrity.

"No other kind of writer risks his neck so visibly or so often on the high wire of public approval," Perelman said of the humorist. "It is the thinnest wire in all literature, and the writer lives with the certain knowledge that he will frequently fall off."[22] One can confidently say that Perelman stayed on that wire longer than any other comic writer in our heritage—half a century. By the time of his death in 1979, the singular regard his fellow professionals always held for him had solidified into formal recognition, like election to the National Institute of

Arts and Letters and being named as the first recipient of the Special
Achievement Award of the National Book Awards Committee.

Perelman gloomily assumed that he was the last of his breed, sole
surviving professional prose humorist—"as a class this type of writer
is doomed"[23]—and he realized that he would soon follow contemporaries like Lardner, Benchley, Thurber, and Groucho into a final
resting place in the pages of anthologies and cultural histories. But
right up to the end, his energy seemed unabated, his acidity quotient
rising higher and higher, his wit unmellowed by the cowardice that
sometimes overtakes the old and famous when they realize that all they
can now hope to hoard up is their reputation. When he presented the
New York Film Critic's screenwriting award to Woody Allen for
Annie Hall, Perelman still located the writer's warrens at MGM "a
mere gallstone's throw from the Commissary,"[24] and the failed project
to transform Dale Carnegie's *How To Win Friends and Influence People*
into a vehicle worthy of Fanny Brice was still the "Edsel of the
entertainment business." He even went on to tell an antisentimental
tale of how Irving Thalberg had tried to ruin the Screenwriter's Guild,
not the sort of reminiscence usually associated with the mild glow of
good fellowship and cigar smoke at rubber-chicken banquets and
awards presentations. Perelman never had any use for smarm; in fact,
the comic mind might be defined as a sensibililty that must do
something about the falsity that the world presents it.

The process was subtle, but Perelman's comic writing became even
a touch more bitter in response to those falsities over the course of his
career. Toward the latter part of his life he expressed more of his own
opinions in his published prose and allowed more realistic observations to take their place alongside his familiar cartoon figures and
stylized, two-dimensional lunacies. The falsities of the world now
provoked a more seriously phrased and sour response. Perelman's
presentation of Ernest Hemingway is a useful illustration to show the
emergence of this Blue Period.

Hemingway—Before and After

Perelman's first African trip in the mid-1950s was written up in
seven parts and called "Dr. Perelman, I Presume, or Small-Bore in

Africa"(collected in *The Rising Gorge*). It is a funny but conventional comic treatment of the trip. The humor here always turns back on its narrator; he is himself the only personality brought low. Perelman arrives with two dozen first-aid nostrums and antivenom kits and finds himself in Kenya during the bloodiest phase of the Mau-Mau racial uprisings. His imperturbable hosts, the veddy British "Mothersills," caution him about the "odd rhino or the unexpected terrorist patrol," and Perelman has himself putting out his cigarette in a dish of wild-currant jam and discovering that his guest room is full of a great many closets he had not noticed before, each and every one of them large enough to "hold a man nursing a grievance."

On the second leg of his trip, Perelman coincidentally crosses paths with the world's most famous writer and his own opposite number: Ernest Hemingway, the great bard of the masculine outdoors, then at the height of his fame. The wire services had reported him killed. In Mark Twain's famous phrase, the reports were greatly exaggerated, and Hemingway was brought to recuperate at the same Stanley Hotel in Nairobi where Perelman was staying. Hemingway's recuperation was materially aided by the enjoyment of reading his own obituaries. Newspapers, of course, have obituaries for all famous people prewritten and waiting for the last moment, and every paper in the world was running one on the great dead American novelist, including a German item that pictured Hemingway's last moments as a Wagnerian suicide plunge, by airplane, into the "crater" of Kilimanjaro. "They're superb—I'll never live up to them"[25] Hemingway told Perelman with a cavalier disdain for the appurtenances of mortality and newspaper trivia that commemorates one's passing—Hemingway playing Hemingway.

From this point on in the pieces, Perelman's comedy centers on his own efforts as a former premed student to help Papa back to health, and Papa is presented precisely as Papa always liked to see himself presented: the very embodiment of reticent courage and "grace under pressure." After all, he was only suffering from a double concussion and a ruptured kidney, and his liver had stopped functioning for just a bit; nothing for a real man to complain about. Perelman of course casts himself as the overcautious four-eyed fussbudget, and he allows his Hemingway to act out the role of a wounded Mercutio who will not let the necessity of drinking medicine get in the way of the pleasure of drinking Campari. This was all strictly according to the party line for presentations of Ernest Hemingway in print, circa 1955. When a tourist-groupie from Milwaukee inveigles Perelman into introducing her to the great man lying injured in his room, there is a mild sort of comic tension between the two writers because the woman, after having persuaded Perelman to introduce her to Hemingway, follows this up by foisting her almost-completed novel on her idol: "'What's more, she graciously offered to let me write a preface for it,'"[26] the novelist exclaimed to Perelman in exasperation. So Perelman is browbeaten into returning the manuscript with appropriate regrets, and the essay more or less peters out with a mysterious and embarrassed disclaimer from its creator as to why he saw so little of Hemingway from that point on: "It was a strange damn thing; there I was on the same floor as Hemingway the rest of that month, and yet somehow we never got together."[27] All in all, Perelman's depiction of Hemingway in this piece is as flattering to the novelist as a photoessay on the man for, say, *Life* would have been— and the Luce enterprises always portrayed Hemingway as the great American writer-hero of this century.

Almost twenty years later, Perelman again returns to the same incident to write about it. Only by 1975, the picture is drawn with darker inks, the tone is acid with spleen and scorn, and now Perelman does not cast himself in the guise of a literary Casper Milquetoast. In fact, Hemingway by this time is on view as the centerfold illustration in Perelman's account of the fatuous male preening himself in an orgy of narcissism and adolescent bravura, and the essay is ominously titled "The Machismo Mystique."[28] By 1975, Hemingway's grace under pressure and wounded-cavalier gallantry have been replaced by some very unflattering mannerisms, neuroses, captions, and comparisons. Now Perelman describes Papa as "unquestionably the holder of the black belt in the Anglo-Saxon world,"[29] for sheer, insufferable male macho, and if Hemingway was still just a pretension or two behind Mike Todd in that department, he is the only male Perelman has ever seen who even comes close. The second time he tells the story, Perelman reveals that Hemingway was not only suffering from the kidney and liver injuries, but that his mind had been affected with "alarming symptoms of *folie de grandeur*,"[30] and now Perelman claims that, far from never getting together with Hemingway during the recuperation at the Stanley Hotel, he "saw a good bit" of the novelist over the weeks. And now Hemingway is not a drinker but a drunk, with his rambling, hallucinatory discourse nothing more than a kind of truck driver's daydream of male bravado. One special anecdote "stunningly dramatized his machismo," Perelman says, and he proceeds to detail an account he had not told us the first time through. This account, violent and puerile to an astonishing degree, concerns Hemingway's brag of some bare-knuckled fistfighting and head-butting free-for-alls he had indulged in at a New York gym. Hemingway and his macho sparring-partner would create a fogbank of live steam by opening the petcock of a radiator, "Then we started charging each other like rhinos. Butting our heads together and roaring like crazy. God, it was terrific. . . . You had to have real *cojones* to stand up to it."[31]

In the same essay Perelman goes on to skewer Robert Ruark ("who of course patterned himself slavishly on Hemingway"), John O'Hara, and, inevitably, Michael Todd, comparing those outsize adolescent male egos unfavorably with two of the men he most admired in his life: Nathanael West and Scott Fitzgerald. It is only in this later, darker, more realistic piece that Perelman reveals to us the fascinating fact that both West and Fitzgerald "were continually obsessed by delusions of their inadequacy with sex and their small literary output."[32] A statement like that one, intimate, adult, responsible, and sympathetic, would have been difficult to associate with the Perelman of the 1940s and 1950s, and we should also notice that the persona he now offers as his alter ego is far less of a standard Milquetoast contraption vibrating with cowardice, petty avarice, and puffery than it has ever been before. And now we also begin to find *tenderness* in Perelman's work, a quality he has hardly ever demonstrated previously—not mellowness, or acceptance, or even simple resignation, but authentic tenderness. Given the source, the effect is sometimes startling—but very welcome. For example, "Mad About the Girl"[33] is an intimate Humbert Humbert confession written by a man of sixty-five who finds himself hopelessly in love: Perelman claims that although he is old enough to be down in Sarasota pitching horseshoes, he has fallen for a very young female. In fact, the female is no more than fifteen months old. Nor is she his granddaughter—this is not a piece written for the *Reader's Digest*.

The young female is a baby gorilla in a Swiss zoo, Quarta by name, and she is "so sweet you could eat her with a spoon."[34] Perelman had read about the birth of the little creature and its three siblings to a female already in captivity, a rarity in the realm of caged gorilladom, and he journeys all the way to Europe just to view it. And when he sees the baby gorilla's mother fondling her tiny offspring in the cage, Perelman's prose reproduces the scene with almost startling eloquence: "as she sat in the cage cuddling it, the benign maternal expression beggared all the religious art in the Uffizi and the Pitti Palace."[35]

Casual as that sort of phrase seems, it is aesthetically very risky to reduce the supreme achievements of Italian Renaissance art to second-best in comparison with a monkey: the fact that Perelman gets away with it, that he effortlessly convinces us of the dignity and beauty of the animals and the bond of love between them, reveals a fresh new appreciation for the powers of realistic description in his approach.

Perelman died in his sleep during the night of October 17, 1979. He had spent the evening of the day before his death at the home of his old friend and fellow *New Yorker* contributor Philip Hamburger, whose elegiac reminiscence for the *Reader's Digest*[36] emphasizes the humorist's punctiliousness in regard to manners, dress, and conversation. Arriving for dinner *precisely* at 7:30 and dressed in peerless tweeds, "the very model of a modern English gentleman," Perelman's correctness sounds to us as monumental as Phileas Fogg's. But Hamburger makes clear that Perelman's "regal manners" and the "immensely dignified" silences were a defense for a deep and abiding shyness. Hamburger also quotes an unnamed young woman's comments on the contrast between Perelman's outward manner, "so crisp and neat and austere," and the enormous responsiveness she discovered just behind that facade: "He seemed almost totally unapproachable until you gained his confidence. From that moment forward, he became a thorough romantic, attentive, observant, confiding. One then felt that one could tell Sid anything, and it would stop with him. He never failed to notice what a woman was wearing, or what jewelry she had put on. In fact, there was little that escaped his notice at any time." Hope Hale Davis also emphasized Perelman's self-imposed limitations in a little reminiscence significantly titled "The Sad Side of Perelman" that appeared after his death. "Unlike [Nathanael West] who with *Miss Lonelyhearts* was able to express the ultimate in compassion, Perelman had let surrealism limit his view of life. I think some of his wildest outside loops spring from the hysteria of a prisoner gone berserk. He had locked himself in his style."[37]

But if posthumous revelations as to Perelman's well-disguised sensitivity and responsiveness do not really surprise us, we might find Hamburger's disclosure of Perelman's supernatural interests truly startling: "Sid had a strong mystical side, an extrasensory area that totally belied his apparently pragmatic approach to life and letters," he recalls, and tells of the evening when Perelman tried to reach the ghost of Robert Benchley via a Ouija board. "I take the Ouija board very seriously," Perelman told Hamburger, braving his friend's embarrassed surprise and making sure that Hamburger understood that these unearthly concerns were not part of a gag. Perhaps because the humorist's career seems dedicated to puncturing illusions and deflating nonsense such an otherworldly disclosure strikes us as out of character; certainly Perelman never made much of these supernatural interests in his published work. But then the distance between Perelman the man and the stylized persona he created for his comic pieces is one of the most intriguing challenges in analyzing his intentions and technique and in assessing his contributions to our literary heritage, and it is to this challenge that we must now turn.

Chapter Four
Perelman and the Tradition
On Falling Out of Fashion

Readers who associate comic prose with good humor and geniality may have been startled at the gritty irritability and uncompromising pessimism Perelman always dished out at interviews, especially since it seemed to clash with our conception of the humorist as a playful fellow. Maralyn Lois Polak spoke to him for the *Philadelphia Inquirer* in 1975, and Perelman fixed her with his "watery blue eyes," and told her that he would freely admit to "all the neuroses and prejudices" attendant upon aging, opined that humor in America has greatly declined since the days of his youth and may not survive at all, and told her that although New York City was "detestable, dangerous, filthy," it at least had a feeling of energy, "a feeling of a pulse around me. Everyone is busy. That's inspiring." As for the process of writing, it had become harder and harder for him: "very time-consuming, painful."[1]

Another interviewer, William Keough of the *Philadelphia Bulletin*, made the mistake of asking Perelman about the future of nothing less than all mankind. "Well," Perelman told him with gleeful nihilism, "we're all headed for extermination . . . it's only a question of when. And I have profound faith in mankind's ability to destroy himself and the earth."[2] How about modern writers? Surely since they reflect the reality of the bomb?—no, definitely not. Sounding like a literary Smedley himself, Perelman proclaimed that contemporary writers "have divorced themselves not only from the past but from reality, they're so far out. I think the drug culture did this. . . ." And so Coover, Barthelme, Pynchon, Tom Robbins, and Brautigan are banished from the bookshelf. "Generally speaking, I don't believe in kindly humor," Perelman once told an interviewer. "One of the most shameful utterances to stem from a human mouth is Will Rogers' 'I never met a man I didn't like.' The absolute antithesis is Oscar Wilde's on the foxhunting Englishman: 'the unspeakable in pursuit of the uneatable.' . . . Wilde's remark contains, in briefest span, the truth; whereas Rogers' is pure flatulence."

Other examples of pure flatulence were the manuscripts on Nathanael West sent to him by hopeful doctoral candidates or enterprising academic *arrivistes*, manuscripts Perelman claimed kept his "incinerator going full time." Nor would he theorize flatulently about his own work: "vaporizing about one's own stylistic intricacies strikes me as being visceral, and to be blunt, inexcusable." He warned off with a growl an interviewer who approached the sacred domain of his writing technique: "What the hell are you trying to extort—my trade secrets?" His pet myna bird was called "Nixon's vulture" in honor of the political figure of that name, and he claimed his impetus to write was a kind of free-floating will to social revenge: "One doesn't consciously start out wanting to be a social satirist," he said, and implied that one is driven to it: "You find something absurd enough to make you want to push a couple of anti-personnel bombs under it. . . ."

Continuing an ancient and honorable line of speculation into the nature of humor, Arthur Koestler has theorized that human laughter may be a sort of alternative satisfaction of "biological drives," a substitute for "killing or copulating," for planting antipersonnel bombs. The aggression implied in laughter—and laughter almost always involves ridicule, bringing low—is "sublimated, often unconscious," but the mechanism of laughter surely involves a psychic effort to reduce or even imaginatively destroy its objects; and we can agree that a good part of the comic phenomenon might be understood as brutality without consequence.

Most humorists detest speculation as to their motives ("only the pedants try to classify it," Perelman put it) for the same reason that most of us do not like to admit to our fascination with gossip: it is not really a very attractive impulse, and jealousy, the largest unacknowledged force in human affairs, always plays a significant part in it. John Lahr theorized that "the comedian gets even with laughter: a hostile sharpshooter using his wit," and Perelman himself said that for *The Beauty Part* he was seeking to puncture the "colossal airs" that the culture-merchandisers and frauds were taking on, that he had consciously set out with a slingful of wit against a Goliath of pretension. And although he said that "humor, in its simplest form, is the unexpected . . . the sudden disruption of thought, the conjoining of unlikely elements," the scientific neutrality of Perelman's formula is sometimes belied by his actual practices; Koestler seems closer to the core of one aspect of comic impulses like Perelman's when he speaks of the "detached malice of the parodist."

But it is important to see that, although he always spoke of himself as a satirist and social picador, Perelman's work does not really address itself to any of the deep concerns and anxieties of the human condition or our historical moment. This is not to say that Perelman did not find himself as involved as any other intelligent man in the fate of his family, city, country, race, species, and planet, for, of course, he did. But it is important to see that his professional writing does not reflect much about those concerns—it is a boredom-fighting machine, not an instrument of social analysis or behavior modification. In T. S. Eliot's famous phrase, "experiences which are important for the man may take no place in the poetry, and those which become important in the poetry may play quite a negligible part in the man, the personality." The fact is that Perelman chose to remain in the camp of those who write with very little direct use of their own full personality and deepest concerns, and this is important to remember in reading him and assessing his place in our literary heritage. Perelman's real difference from the novelists who were his contemporaries may well lie more in the uses they made of their own personalities and the uses he chose *not* to make of his than in the size of their respective works. Fitzgerald, Faulkner, Hemingway, and Nabokov filled each and every page of their fiction with giant images of themselves and their most intimate concerns; younger writers like Mailer, Bellow, Updike, and Roth might even be said to have gone beyond them in projecting themselves onto the page.

In contrast, Perelman is a thin, narrowly focused beam of laser light, drawing power from only one small aspect of his personality and leaving much unused. As Louis Hasley pointed out in an article for the *South Atlantic Quarterly* he calls "The Kangaroo Mind of S. J. Perelman," we find his pieces "harboring no Swiftean anger and revealing no hope of changing things for the better. One may even be tempted to feel he is glad things are as they are. . . ." The true satirist, fully engaged in his attack, cannot be described in those terms, and although Perelman, the man, may have felt the same outrage that drove Swift to write "A Modest Proposal," Twain to savage the slave-lynching Southerner in *Huckleberry Finn*, Evelyn Waugh to saw Hollywood in half for *The Loved One*, or Philip Roth to flay the thirty-seventh president of the United States as "Trick E. Dixon" in *Our Gang*, he did not turn that feeling into professional prose. Nowhere in his work do we find the "fury of derision" or the "killing laughter"—laughter as weaponry—which theorists like Robert C. Elliott find characteristic of that comedy-with-a-purpose we call satire.

Slight in itself, a shift in literary decorum may signify something as fundamental as a shift in the way we choose to think about ourselves: our taste in literature is a seismographic needle recording deep changes in the national consciousness. I would have to agree that Perelman's work is "dated," but I would hasten to add in the same statement that (1) this dating was caused by forces far beyond Perelman's control and stems from the enormous changes history has wrought in those of us who approach his work, and not from deficiencies in the work itself; and (2) the dating of his work is merely a neutral scientific reality, not a judgment of its merit. In a literary era peopled with Erica Jong, Tom Robbins, Xaveria Hollander, Bruce Jay Friedman, and Robert Coover, Perelman, whose comic pieces appeared in the *New Yorker* from 1934 through 1979, does indeed take on some aspects of a beloved anachronism. And, expressed or merely implied, contemporary critical opinion seems to find Perelman belonging rather more in the past than the present. For example, Richard Freedman writes in *Book World*: "The sad fact is that Perelman—or maybe his peculiar genre—is rather irrelevant and dated. A sense of strain, a clutching for effect does mark these pieces [off] from the mainstream of recent humor, which tends to be cooler, more casual, less uptight, and above all, more public."

We might surmise that "more public" is a code equivalent for "less elitist" and simply reject Freedman's criticism as unarguable: after all, Perelman's wit *is* elitist, obviously and triumphantly and right down to its marrow, a specialized and courtly art aimed at a very few, and to argue against it on that score is to involve oneself in those enormously long and complicated, and ultimately insoluable, controversies about the function of art in relation to society.

But Freedman is right (although perhaps for the wrong reasons) when he finds Perelman's things marked off from the "mainstream of recent humor," and it is our obligation to see by how much and why if we are to properly establish Perelman's contribution to our national literature and make some predictions as to how well his work will survive the future. Times change, and critical judgment is responsible for telling us how fast and in which direction.

When *The Beauty Part* was revived for the production in 1974, a dozen years after its first, ill-fated incarnation, only the *ancien régime* of critical assayers welcomed it again—Edith Oliver called it (in the *New Yorker*) the "Return of a Winner"[13] ("the best of all possible worlds," as she paraphrases Candide's Dr. Pangloss in praise of the play), and John McCarten wrote that "A good deal of it shows Mr. Perelman at the top of his game, and when he's there he's a hard man to touch." But younger critics like Dick Brakenfield in the *Village Voice* claimed that the author was "merely playing the role of Perelman the peppery picador of pretentiousness,"[14] and that even the great, all-purpose, all-damning accusation of the post-Vietnam era could be brought against him: insincerity. According to Brakenfield, Perelman's blasts of satiric buckshot "plink off the surface because his projectiles are too verbal. It's magazine stuff lifted onto the stage without a proper rebirth. The angry, living edge is neither fresh nor sharp enough."

The assumptions underlying the rhetoric here are that Perelman needs to be angry and needs to be armed, and especially that he needs to be moving against a foe worthy of his anger and his weapons—a foe we can safely assume this type of critic would have no difficulty recommending to a playwright. However awkwardly phrased, though, a statement like the one just quoted does give us an insight into an important change in our literary expectation and response.

In order to assess Perelman in relation to the present and hazard some guesses as to what the future may do about him, it is first necessary to keep in mind that in some aspects of his work Perelman continues in a very subtle form a European and New World Jewish tradition, and this influence will enrich and complicate our assessment in about equal measure.

Barbershop and *Shlemiel*

Perelman has characterized the state of humor at about the time of his own birth as exhibiting a "barbershop mentality" (and remember that the barbershop and the saloon are the two great male preserves of the nineteenth and early twentieth centuries); and he speaks of the comic prose of that era as "gray and pulpy," with the typical purveyor of that comic prose not the gifted George Ade, Ring Lardner, or Robert Benchley (each of whom Perelman admires), but the cracker-barrel newspaper columnist or barfly sportswriter, "a jackanapes with upturned hatbrim chewing his cigar and relentlessly spouting yocks."[15] This cracker-barrel humorist was the dominant comic role in American writing from about the end of the Civil War to the beginning of World War I, a period of approximately fifty years: long enough to breed a powerful reaction to itself.

Although only literary archeologists can readily identify the names Charles Farrar Browne (1834–67), David Ross Locke (1833–88), and Henry W. Shaw (1818–85), they are almost household names, at least to literary people, when we list their respective noms de plume: Artemus Ward, Petroleum Vesuvius Nasby, and Josh Billings. In each case the comic persona these writers projected was a cleverly manufactured and highly stylized role that became a national literary and show-business style: the shrewd (but not formally educated) countryman whose honest common sense allowed him to see through the hypocrisy and cant of those Eastern city slickers, money-handlers, and windbag politicians. Such a persona, buoyed up by the needs of the community for a literary equivalent of what it wanted to believe about itself, held an obvious appeal for a rural nation only recently a frontier, and within at least a few living memories, a British crown colony. But as with all literary styles, the center would not hold. History always makes new styles necessary.

It is a commonplace to point out that enormous social changes took place in America between about 1865 and 1917, and that these raw changes in the way that Americans lived—indeed, in who Americans *were*—eventually expressed themselves in reshaping American literary motifs. So overfamiliar has the idea become through its sheer repetition that we have ceased to be amazed by it. And yet the change was amazing—for it was nothing less than a transformation of American culture. The first transcontinental railroad was completed in 1869, and this achievement allowed both agricultural and industrial growth to accelerate exponentially; electrical power became widely available to further speed that growth; the telephone revolutionized human communication and everything we associate with Thomas Edison's genius altered America and the rest of the world, once and for all. America was the future—or so it told itself. By the time that Perelman's father had immigrated to America—the land of opportunity—the recent colony was suddenly itself a minor imperialist power—thus followed the Spanish-American War of 1898, where Joseph Perelman saw the sharks devouring the bodies of those American sailors killed in the mine explosion that sank the *Maine*.

Even the elder Perelman's very presence in this country was in itself a result of the enormous wave of immigration created by the needs of America's burgeoning new industrialism: he was himself part of the change. Born in 1904 America and the son of immigrants, then, S. J. Perelman's work would be both a continuation of, and yet a contrast to, a certain comic inheritance, a special tradition.

In talking about people, the persistent difficulty is in separating what is specific to an individual from what is general to a class—and since no one wants to be regarded as merely a product of his background, the ice gets very thin indeed when we generalize about him from only a sociological perspective. Further, the persona that a writer projects may well bear his own name, but that persona is never quite the same thing as the man himself, even when the writer is most assiduous in pretending that it is. Irving Goffman sets out a general warning for the uncritical to be wary of such a confusion: "The [comic or satiric] persona again is not to be considered an aspect or revelation of the author but an independent creation designed for its function as part of the self-contained work . . . the author pretends to be himself, but acts a calculated role. . . ."[16] We must of course not speak of Perelman the character within one of his own stories as if he were the mirror-image of Perelman the writer, for with such a highly stylized prose cartoonist it is axiomatic that we have to be cautious in equating the human being with the created character. But one is not obliged to subscribe without question to the purity of the New Criticism—to consciously exclude a writer's personality from his work, to study only the words he gives us on the printed page. Like all writers, Perelman works out of a set of constant concerns and with certain idiosyncratic techniques. One aspect of these constant concerns in Perelman's work is a touch of the sensibility we have come to associate with American Jews. The strand we might characterize as minor, but still somewhat important. In contrast to other Jewish writers, he keeps it quite muted. But it is not entirely absent, and Perelman would be a slightly different sort of writer if he were not a part, however tangential a part, of what we might caption "the Jewish-American sensibility." This special inheritance played a part in Perelman's reaction to the tradition he found holding sway as he formed his literary sensibility.

A pair of quotations from two Jewish critics can help summarize the label we are attempting to attach to Perelman's name.

Irving Howe has preserved in English some observations made in Yiddish by the critic Ba'al Makhshoves; these were made by a European Jew, of course, and he was also speaking of a ghetto population struggling to survive within the repressive Russia of the Czars. Still, Makhshoves's comments are not unhelpful when we come to observe Perelman's work.

The individual Jewish sensibility that is formed in the ghetto, Makhshoves points out, derives from a small, helpless, closed-off society that is utterly paralyzed by police authority and the iron ring of the surrounding social antipathy that bears down upon it; by its extreme material poverty; and by its special historic devotion to things not of this world—that is, by its self-chosen spiritual attention to the invisible kingdom of belief that has always set it out against each and every host society all through the millenial nighttime ages of the Dispersion. Sight, hearing, touch, smell, taste all diminish in consequence of the conditions. The ghetto society is free-floating, almost ghostly, perhaps even a little hallucinatory from sheer hunger and ennui, and sustains itself on the spectral claims and promises of the sacred text, the Torah. "But among [the Jew's] atrophied senses there remained vivid only the sixth one," Makhshoves claims, "an overly sharp intelligence which tended to laugh and jeer at the contradictions of the life he was leading. . . ." The Jew develops "a sharply critical intelligence that hangs suspended over a dead body [and] feels the agonies of life as though in a dream." As a defense against his humiliation, the Jew develops a special voice, "The voice of self-contempt. . . . In Jewish mockery one can hear . . . the sick despair of a people whose existence has become an endless array of contradictions, a permanent witticism."[17] The Jew can never fit in, that is his curse and his gift, and yet he must experience the endless and dangerous consequences of this refusal and self-chosen alienation from the dominant culture.

Robert Alter is the second Jewish critic whose comments are relevant to Perelman's comic heritage and achievement. If Makhshoves's observations describe a purgatorial European ghetto world which survives only vestigially in the racial memories of an American-Jewish writer, Alter's comments touch much closer to the heritage Perelman must have found immediately about him in his childhood and youth. "Writers significantly touched by the Yiddish heritage," Alter suggests, "have often been de-mythologizers, using the wryness and homey realism of Jewish humor to suggest a less melodramatic, less apocalyptic, perspective than that of myth might be appropriate for viewing even the disquieting state of affairs of the modern world."[18] For all its fantastic comedy and frequently surreal recombinations, Perelman's comic forays do not create systems of illusion or alternative worlds we can really believe in; instead, they call attention to the absurdities of the real world by means of exaggerating them to such outlandish size that we cannot help but finally notice. The comic writer is not usually a sustainer, a daydreamer in the service of his readers, he is essentially a deflater, a flattener, and his antics work to restore clear common sense: Louis Hasley speaks for many others when he says that Perelman's "balance wheel" is reason itself, and he describes Perelman's comic method as the "reasoned absurd."[19] John Updike once made the wonderful observation that every true story has an anticlimax. As the mode of thought and perception built around the anticlimax, comedy is by its very nature a means of reducing fiction to fact, of distilling crystals of reality out of frothy alembics of hokum and romantic illusion. Perelman is a legatee of the Yiddish and American-Jewish tradition, and for the last two thousand years no Jew could afford to be unrealistic about the Christian culture that surrounds him. It is no accident that Perelman's style of thought shows residual traces of a heritage that has always stood outside the central myths of any culture in which it rather precariously found itself afloat. Thus, the pioneer mythology and the West-winning braggadocio, the tall tale and the wise countryman whose plainspun words and observations are couched in a vocabulary and coordinated by a grammar that consciously scorn "book learnin' " and sophisticated reference—these are the properties and devices we *never* find in Perelman, and his Jewish heritage may well have assisted his personal choice against these forms.

Speaking in general of Jewish writers, Mark Shechner says that "as immigrant, emigré, displaced person, or holder of dual citizenship, the Jew finds the correct interpretation of foreign signs a vital part of his daily routine, and has been obliged historically to turn the hyphen in his identity into the cutting edge of a sharp sensibility. . . . amphibians that they are, Jews are experts in incongruity."[20] But of course if Perelman is an expert's expert in incongruity—incongruity is after all the essence of his career—it is important to notice that the absurdities of which he writes are almost always intrinsically trivial. Thus, we might allow that Perelman's mental stance is Jewish insofar as it is alert to incongruity and alive to the comic possibilities inherent in unmasking fakery and cant, but that the very triviality of his chosen subject matter—all those hundreds of parodies of advertising puffery, those send-ups of bad movies, those epic weekend struggles with the E-Z Jiffy Portable Closet that one is supposed to be able to assemble with a half-dozen staples in five minutes—seems hardly the sort of incongruity that we would associate with the preoccupations of a literate Jew in our century. We can never forget that for any Jew living through this era there is an incongruity so large and terrible that the mind can hardly surround it, and that is the fact of Auschwitz. The Nazi death camps made it impossible for one to add as an afterthought that such-and-such a writer "happens to be a Jew"—as we might say that of a writer that happens to be a Canadian, or a

Southerner, or a physician, or one who went to Princeton. To be a Jew is to be defined, once and for all, by one's identity with the six million who were consumed, to understand that one's very physical life depended solely on *that* connection and no other. This is a large absurdity, perhaps not least of all because it makes the individual personality irrelevant, for it is an unpleasant necessity to have to acknowledge that one's life or death, to say nothing of one's personal sense of worth, trembles on the scales of a single and arbitrary fact: one's Jewishness. Mark Harris supplies us with a useful short-hand notation for the qualities we might find common to almost all Jewish writers after the Holocaust when he remarks this of Saul Bellow (surely the most honored of all American-Jewish authors): "Life, peace, and civilization he favored, guns and untimely death he opposed. Historian, humorist, Jewish, American. A political radical, seeing the world whole, true anti-fascist. . . ."[21]

It might even be claimed that if we were asked to link with a common denominator Jewish-American writers as various as Bellow, Richard Stern, J. D. Salinger, Norman Mailer, Philip Roth, Bernard Malamud, E. L. Doctorow, and Bruce Jay Friedman, Harris's cluster of attributes would be a good place to begin. The cattle cars, gas chambers, and firing squads of the Final Solution defined a person's right to live by a single measure, and that incongruity has lent to Jewish writing its special qualities of tragic irony, sensitivity to the absurd, and humanistic dismay. For example, Bellow's Artur Sammler has lost his wife and the sight of one eye to the Nazi SS, was shot and left for dead under a pile of Jewish corpses in 1945, and has survived into an old age and an historical moment he can only find amazing, dangerous, luridly fascinating, and charged with moral irony. Allowed by sheer dumb luck to live on as a man reprieved from the dead, knowing the worst and yet with a spark of optimism still unextinguished in him, Sammler of necessity desperately tries to make sense of the human scene he finds before him. "Oh, what a wretched, itching, bleeding, needing, idiot, genius of a creature we are dealing with here,"[22] Sammler's mind shouts to itself, and it would be difficult not to find a mind-cry so contradictory and cosmic, so shocked and hopeful and intense anywhere outside the pages of a Jewish writer.

However difficult to isolate and define, the family resemblance we find among Jewish writers is powerfully real: taken as a group, their emotional pitch oscillates between registers both higher and lower, more idealistic and more despairing than any other group of imaginations we might gather under one sociological label. Speculation on nothing less than the human condition is Sammler's obsession—because he was almost murdered for no good reason at all, Sammler (like all of Bellow's alter egos) can never stop trying to comprehend the energies which animate a world which offers up such a spectacle of tenderness and violence, suffering and sensitivity and brutality.

Even J. D. Salinger, a writer less overtly Jewish and one less interested in the sociological classification of his characters, has furnished us with several unforgettable images of the mind of a sensitive observer reeling with shock at man's inhumanity to man as exemplified by the Nazi destruction centers. Seymour Glass in "A Perfect Day for Bananafish" has returned from the European Theater of Operations with a head full of images he cannot exorcise—or can exorcise only by means of a 7.65 millimeter automatic bullet. The Sergeant X of "For Esmé—with Love and Squalor" has arrested several Nazi officials and, it is implied, discovered for himself the horrifying reality of the Final Solution: dirty and disheveled, chain-smoking and with his gums bleeding from lack of vitamin C, unable to write a legible sentence or read the letters accumulating on his desk from the wife, family, and friends stateside (after all, they have not accompanied him down through the Inferno), Sergeant X finds his mind about to give way: "abruptly, familiarly, and, as usual, with no warning, he thought he felt his mind dislodge itself and teeter, like insecure luggage on an overhead rack."[23]

Sergeant X's sanity is saved by his receipt of a gift of pure generous love from Esmé, her dead father's wristwatch, but it has been a very close call—a melodrama of betrayed humanism. E. L. Doctorow's harrowing fictionalization of the Rosenberg electrocutions portrays the McCarthy-era United States as virulently anti-Semitic as Russia under the czars, and Bernard Malamud's brand of Jewish humor makes a startling and instructive contrast with Perelman's lightweight and cautiously nonethnic pieces—Malamud's fairy tales and fables, touched most everywhere with a sort of fey but melancholy surrealism something in the manner of prose equivalents of Marc Chagall stained glass, are characterized by what Robert Alter calls the paradox of "immense sadness of matter and [yet a] delightfulness of manner," and create a peculiarly Jewish paradox, "the use of comedy as a last defense of the imagination against grim fate."[24]

Few books are at once funnier or more serious than Philip Roth's *Portnoy's Complaint*, surely the most exhaustive account we have on that uniquely Jewish conflict between the ethical and the impulsive, the ought-to-be and the actual. And Isaac Bashevis Singer, perhaps the greatest of all the Yiddish-language writers, always bent his comedy toward nothing less ambitious than the ageless problems of human consciousness trying to make sense of the world that encloses it, flirts with it, and finally puts it to death: "No doubt the world is an entirely imaginary world," Singer's Gimpel the Fool muses, "but it is only once removed from the true world." In short, Perelman stands a good deal away from the mainstream of what we have come to recognize as Jewish literary concerns. But can we look to his times and milieu to find a clue why? My answer would be that we can, and that the connection between Perelman and his times and heritage is both more significant and more subtle than it at first appears.

Looked at from the point of view of historical tendency, Perelman's work might best be approached as a composite of three strains of sensibility we can isolate in the American-Jewish immigrant culture of his time: (1) the intense desire to assimilate into the culture of WASP America, an enthusiasm in making haste toward the sociological "melting pot" which we in our era might find alarming, embarrassing, or naive; (2) an intense Jewish-cultural reverence for words and works of literature (and its inevitable counterreflex, a revulsion against their defilement or misuse); and (3) a sensitivity to the surrounding world of power and significance that emphasizes its hypocrisy, its double standards and evasions, and its reluctance to face the truth.

Although he noted that his own style made use of "liberal doses of Yiddish," Perelman did not mean to indicate by that claim that he was in any sense an ethnic or dialect comic writer—we may even be sure such a description would have undoubtedly provoked his famous temper. And even if one concedes that his use of Yiddish may demonstrate a wry affection for his heritage (remember that his father had once backed an unsuccessful effort to transform Scott's *The Heart of Midlothian* into a Yiddish musical), his appropriation of that language actually seems less of a tribute than an expedient. The "invective content" of Yiddish is very high, Perelman once claimed, pointing out that he could count no fewer than nineteen distinct Yiddish words that indicated gradations of disparagement. But this is hardly the sort of respectful tone we have come to associate with the evocation of ethnic roots. In fact, as a type, the Jewish artist or entertainer of Perelman's era and background—the children of Eastern European immigrants born here in America before World War I—almost always seem to have demonstrated a richly ambivalent attitude toward his or her Jewish cultural heritage. Their fame and their gifts were immense, but the names by which the world knows them—Jack Benny, George and Ira Gershwin, Eddie Cantor, Paul Muni, George Jessel, Sophie Tucker, Milton Berle, Ben Hecht, Irving Berlin, Ben Blue, Sammy Cahn, Ted Lewis, George Burns, Fanny Brice, Dorothy Parker, Sid Caesar, Al Jolson, for example—were in many cases not even the names they were born with. At least to some extent, these Jews were in disguise. This cultural self-disguising and impersonation was evidently not easy to live with, and Irving Howe makes a subtle point superbly when he speculates that, in the mouth of an older comedian or entertainer, one whose career had begun with a denial or suppression of his own heritage, "a rough splatter of Yiddish could become a way of suggesting that they knew they were in the service of unworthy ends. . . . [Their new] stage and screen bilingualism [now] refracted a moral duality, spilling contempt on Jews, themselves not least of all, for being inauthentic and on gentiles for rewarding them. . . . From the earlier anxiety to please—the please at all costs: self-denial, self-effacement, self-exhaustion—the humor of the Jewish entertainers moved, through the passage of generations, toward a rasping aggressiveness, an arrogant declaration of a despised Jewishness."[25] Very late in his career a trace of this aggression began to show up in Perelman's work, but it seems important to notice that he rarely made use of his own Jewishness or of the comic possibilities of Jewishness as a comic situation at any point in his career—a career that spanned almost fifty professional years.

Perhaps we can best approach his use of a smattering of Yiddish words (most of them widely understood, in fact, like *nudnik*, or *chutzpah*) as simple wordplay, a bit of comic foolery we should not confuse with the humor of cultures in collision. Perelman might even be described as a Jewish writer ill at ease with Jewishness—a writer neither celebrating nor exploiting his cultural heritage. This does not mean that his sensibility bears no trace of what we have come to call the American-Jewish sensibility; there is in fact more of the subcultural in Perelman's work than he would have comfortably acknowledged. But his case is subtle.

"Insofar as the work of the American Jewish writer bears a relationship to the Jewish past," Howe claims, "it is mostly mediated through the historical phase of Yiddish. . . . But even the relationship of [strictly traditional and ethnic] writers to the culture of Yiddish, source and root of their early experience, is marked by rupture, break, dissociation, by a will to flee, and, once and for all, be done with."[26] This "will to flee" from the ethnic trappings and properties of Jewishness is surely appropriate in describing Perelman's work, but then the will to flee, or, really, the will to rise, was a significant impulse in Yiddish culture at large. Millions of Jews did not come to America with the expectation that they were always to remain Old World Yiddish-speaking Jews; and from the beginning the Yiddish-speaking community in America showed every symptom of a subculture riven by energies it could neither contain, redirect, or satisfy. Yiddish theater is a case in point. Regular performances at permanent venues began to be offered to the immigrant community in the 1880s; these performances must have appeared to the immigrant audiences as one of the New World's most startling phenomena, for theatricality and secular plays had been for centuries sternly condemned by the religious leaders of the European Diaspora, and the few professional groups of acrobats and singers that wandered the countryside were ragamuffin troupes only a step ahead of destitution. Although the opposition of the Orthodox community was so intense that the very first New York production of a Yiddish play (Abraham Goldfaden's *The Sorceress*, "an operetta in 5 acts and 9 tableaux") almost failed before the curtain went up, Yiddish-language theater soon prospered, and then, after reaching a peak of about twenty theaters in operation during World War I, continued on in some form for more than twenty-five years before it finally disintegrated as a significant institution.

Perelman once described his own style in a manner that suggests we might even find in it something of the same tensions between high art and slapstick, culture and trash, that marks the drama of that time. "My style is mélange," Perelman said. "A mixture of all the sludge I read as a child, all the clichés, liberal doses of Yiddish, criminal slang, and some of what I was taught in a Providence, Rhode Island school by impatient teachers." Yiddish-language productions were equally strange amalgamations of clownish claptrap and high ideas, "sludge" and revered drama. Like Perelman's pieces, they were at once self-indulgent and yet uneasy with that self-indulgence, like children who have gorged themselves on too much candy. Joseph Lateiner and "Professor" Morris Horowitz (a self-bestowed title with which he hoped to overawe his immigrant audience) concocted more than two hundred plays which compressed together stories from the Old Testament, topical references (to the czarist repressions in Russia, for example), family melodrama, Shakespearean plots like *Romeo and Juliet* recast into Jewish situations, vaudeville turns and disconnected soliloquies, and a great deal of musical comedy. But if the unlettered immigrant masses who attended these productions found them eminently satisfactory, many of the actors and playwrights responsible for offering such fare wanted to do better. Jewish culture always *aspires*, and its ideals are very high indeed. The actor and producer David Kessler spoke poignantly of the conflict he felt between easy success with vulgar *shund*, "trash," and artistic conscience—one might even call it the central crisis of conscience for the Jewish entertainer of our century: "*Shund* is more profitable. I must do plays that attract the public if I'm going to pay the rent. But when I play trash it's like drinking castor oil."[27]

The playwrights who succeeded hacks like Lateiner and Horowitz, among them Sholem Asch, David Pinski, Ossip Bymov, and Peretz Hirschein, desperately tried to transform or at least imitate serious world drama and conjured with names like Ibsen, Shaw, Galsworthy, Chekov, Tolstoy, and Hauptmann, but almost all of these well-meant attempts toward high theatrical culture failed at the box office. Even the famous Yiddish Art Theatre, founded by Maurice Schwartz just after World War I, found itself compelled to present folksy genre pieces and sentimental marriage comedies in order to survive, although it had hoped to offer Moliére and Shakespeare and Strindberg and the most promising of contemporary experiments. From the outset, Jewish intellectuals could not and would not leave Yiddish theater to its music-hall skits, knockabout comics in spirit-gum whiskers, and sentimental claptrap. Maurice Schwartz himself, although responsible for more than 150 productions before the Yiddish Art Theatre disbanded in 1950, could never reconcile the conflicting claims of unpolished folk comedy with his aspirations to elevate Yiddish-language plays to a respectable place in *velt kultur*, world culture, and we might view his efforts in retrospect as a microcosm of the schizophrenia that afflicted and finally destroyed the Yiddish culture of that era. As Howe phrases it, the leaders of the Yiddish theatrical phenomenon could never be content with merely satisfying the "unwashed plebes," rescuing a moment of mirth and brightness for lives "lost forever in the darkness of the sweatshop."[28] If it was true that, as Brooks Atkinson drily observed of the Yiddish theater, "you always knew you were not in a library," no other ethnic theater in our national experience was ever more thoroughly conscience-bedeviled into finding its own métier unsatisfactory when measured against its aspirations. Obviously Perelman and other university-educated Jews of that era recognized early on that Yiddish culture was in itself a dead end, but the path they chose up and out of it was in itself markedly "Jewish," perhaps especially in its comic and satiric elements and in its attitudes toward established propriety and power.

In order to show how Perelman's career as a humorist was but one example of a broader sociological tendency we might look at the parallels between his progress and that of George S. Kaufman, beyond all comparison the most successful Jewish comic writer of the time.

Kaufman was born in Pittsburgh in 1889, and his father, like Perelman's, was something of a rolling stone who turned restlessly from one business to another; money was as much of a problem in the Kaufman household as it was as the Perelmans'. Just as with Perelman, one of the most obvious legacies the elder Kaufman left to his son was his liberal and humane politics and social philosophy—in fact, at his death in 1940, Kaufman's father left his last enterprise, a silk-dyeing company, to his employees rather than to his family, and he had long before been one of the first employers of his time to insist that his work-force put in no more than forty hours a week. Like Perelman, Kaufman began his career as a journalist, sold humor to the magazines while still in his teens, and wrote a great many odds and ends for various stage revues before achieving his first installment of fame and fortune—dazzling fame and enormous fortune—with his comedy *Dulcy* (a collaboration with Marc Connelly) in 1921. Like Perelman, Kaufman was an enormously hard worker and meticulous wordsmith who would spend an afternoon polishing one line. Both were *New Yorker* contributors from its inception. Like Perelman, Kaufman's first marriage was devoted, and loving, and both writers at times collaborated on professional work with their wives (and for whatever it is worth, Beatrice Bakrow Kaufman bore a startling physical resemblance to Laura West Perelman). Both men loathed Hollywood but journeyed there for the lucre and both had Bucks County retreats (Kaufman, like Perelman unable to resist a pun, called his "Cherchez la Farm"). Kaufman always claimed that he never wanted to be anywhere where he could not get back to Times Square in half an hour, and Perelman never felt at home anywhere other than Manhattan Island. Kaufman was of course a central figure in the most famous *ad hoc* social institution of the American 1920s, the Algonquin Round Table; and Perelman, although his credentials for "membership" in that salon were impeccable, most emphatically was not—but even here we might chalk up the dissimilarity to simply personal style and needs, for Kaufman was a more gregarious social type, almost always collaborated on his theatrical projects (with an astonishing sixty-six different scripts), and loved to play high-stakes bridge or poker in his leisure time. But central to our comparison, of course, is the similarity of their comic point of view. Both are comic writers first, disappointed liberals second. Both are more interested in amusing than instructing. Here Kaufman's most famous effort is perhaps his most representative, the 1931 Broadway smash musical *Of Thee I Sing.*

The play is a mild and playful satire on American politics, and the fatuousness of the presidential race is presented with a bumptious energy that can still amuse even in our time. The bachelor candidate for his party's nomination, John P. Wintergreen, cynically arranges for a marriage with the winner of an Atlantic City beauty contest—only a happily married man could ever be elected to the presidency, of course, and America, as we all know, loves a lover. The plan backfires when Wintergreen, after being elected, spurns the Southern belle who has been chosen to win; and since the girl is of French ancestry, America finds itself on the brink of war with France over the insult. (The gibes were in fact so effective and unflattering that the French government really did protest.) Of course everything works out by the curtain, but the cynicism directed toward the American political process is thoroughgoing before the plot is finally tied up. As Kaufman's biographer Scott Meredith put it, the musical's target was "a formerly forbidden subject, the shameless pandering of politicians to racial, religious, and other special-interest groups."[29] Nor was the "common man" flattered or the superpatriot spared: presidential votes go to Mickey Mouse and Mae West. A fathead senator argues for a pension for that dear old quadruped hero, Paul Revere's horse. "Heavenly funny," one contemporary reviewer noted, "but also serious as hell." Another called it "the most intelligent, the most consistent, the most timely satire of American politics the native theatre has entertained."[30] As a product of its times, it is significant to notice that although four Jews had collaborated in the creation of the musical—Kaufman and Morrie Ryskind took care of the plot and prose, George and Ira Gershwin the music and lyrics—the play has no Jewish characters at all. Real-life Jews of Kaufman's and Perelman's generation insisted on being regarded as first of all Americans—were in fact anxious not to appear narrow and ethnic. And as mild as it is, *Of Thee I Sing* is in essence a response to disappointment as well as a comedy in and of itself: its satirical, corrective strain is an attempt to poke the body politic into doing what it ought to be doing, a concern that we associate with Jewish culture and its moral conscience from Karl Marx on through J. Robert Oppenheimer. Uneasiness with established power and concern with hypocrisy on the part of social institutions has long been a concern of Jews, for so many centuries and in so many countries victimized by the central order. Kaufman's play, like so much Jewish comedy, speaks comically but carries a stick—or at least a pin. And even if Perelman's concerns were usually more aesthetic, playful, and apolitical than were Kaufman's, it would not be a difficult stretch of the imagination to see him as the author of a piece of work similar to *Of Thee I Sing* or, if George S. Kaufman had not existed, feel that Perelman's writing for the stage might have played a larger part in his career. The essential affinity of texture and tone is certainly not just a forced parallel, and William Zinsser's comment of Perelman could be applied equally as well to Kaufman: both of them "Startle us with nonsense into seeing our lives with sense." Comedy, Jewish comedy most emphatically, recalls us to a sense of what ought to be. It deflates, demythologizes, almost never the reverse.

In his analysis of Perelman's work for the Marx brothers, J. A. Ward makes the rather large claim that Perelman's style "obviously derives from the basic form of American Jewish monologue, the *shpritz*"[31]—the *shpritz* being a kind of free-form eruption of fantasy, nonsense, and satire, at least theoretically spontaneous and gathering momentum as it goes. In its extreme form, as with the late Lenny Bruce, the *shpritz* becomes a sort of public psychiatric confession: in its essence, it is corrective, morally outraged, but sometimes even more dangerous to its wielder than to the objects of attack. Albert Goldman's harrowing account of Bruce's descent into heroin and self-destruction emphasizes the comedian's authenticity as "a genuine folk-artist," articulating attitudes and sharing anxieties peculiar to American Jews, with the monologue form itself deriving from the Brooklyn street-corner variety of adolescent raillery, those "sessions of ritualistic parody in which [the teenaged Jews] vented their contempt for the life around them."[32]

But if Lenny Bruce is a striking example of Jewish disappointment turned outward into social chastisement, that same anxiety turned inward, the *shpritz* employed as an instrument of masochism rather than of sadism, is perhaps best exemplified by the comic self-lacer-ations of Woody Allen. It is in fact with Allen's comedic style that we come closest to finding an analogue with Perelman's. And if the idea of the *shpritz* is helpful in understanding the cultural backdrop to their comedy, the figure of the *shlemiel* is even more illuminating.

Although Leo Rosten speaks of the *shlemiel* as simply a foolish person, a simpleton and victim, "a clumsy, butterfingered, all-thumbs gauche type,"[33] the figure is not so passive and one-dimensional. As Ruth R. Wisse points out in her study of the evolution of this distinctly Jewish archetype, the *shlemiel* should not be confused with the *shlimazl*, the real passive victim, who "happens on mischance."[34] The *shlemiel* confronts and transforms the misfortune that befalls him: his "misfortune is his character. It is not accidental, but essential. . . . [His] comedy is existential, deriving from his very nature in its confrontation with reality." The *shlemiel's* transformation of fear into farce, is, she argues, the perfect embodiment of Freud's theoretical claim that humor is a *defensive* process, "a means of drawing the energy from the release of unpleasure that is already in preparation and of transforming it, by discharge, into pleasure."[35] The *shlemiel* understands the grim inevitability of his fate; he is anything but brainless, naive, or unworldly, and laughs to keep himself from tears. Thus, a Yiddish joke has the *shlemiel* standing aside and laughing while the rest of his family rushes to put out the fire that is consuming his hovel; asked angrily what he is laughing at, the *shlemiel* replies that he is at least witnessing his revenge on the cockroaches.

Irving Howe points out that Woody Allen's use of the bumbling and incapable but endlessly aware persona of the *shlemiel*, that quintessential Jewish witness-victim, "exploited the parochial helplessness of Jewish sons, their mutual feelings of sexual feebleness and worldly incapacity."[36] Wistful and watery-eyed, muttering to us that his sex life has just been purchased by Parker Brothers to be made into a game, Allen-as-*shlemiel* is merely the latest incarnation of the Jew who tries to come to terms with his victimization via the comedy of self-contempt. But if he himself is incapable, the *shlemiel* implies to us that the world around him is brutal, and, therefore, worse than he is. Wisse points out that representative *shlemiel* humor employs "both the contempt of the strong for the weak and the contempt of the weak for the strong, with the latter winning the upper hand."[37] In a larger sense, the Jewish fool is seen to be right, she claims. "Outrageous and absurd as his innocence may be by the normal guidelines of political reality, the Jew is simply rational within the context of ideal humanism. He is a fool, seriously—maybe even fatally—out of step with the actual march of events."[38] We should also remind ourselves that the figure achieved such resonance in Jewish culture not merely because the Jews were victims for so long but because, of all cultures, Jews have surely been the most thoroughly nonviolent, the most uneasy with the sources of irrationality in human nature. Allen and Perelman both adapt the *shlemiel* to their purposes (Allen more than Perelman), but it is in terms of prose style that the similarity is most marked. In his written work Allen is a frank imitator of Perelman's. Here in its entirety (and suspicious familiarity) is an entry from Allen's "hitherto secret private journal": "I have decided to break off my engagement with W. She doesn't understand my writing, and said last night that my *Critique of Metaphysical Reality* reminded her of *Airport*. We quarreled, and she brought up the subject of children again, but I convinced her they would be too young."[39]

One does not want to bear down too hard on a passage like this, but it may not be quite like breaking butterflies on the wheel to point out that the parody here is not only phrased with Perelman cadences, but also that it is funny because it is grounded in betrayed *intellectual* expectations. The humor smacks of an Ivy League graduate school. And if Allen's comedy always evokes the figure of the *shlemiel* in its foreground, in its background we might catch a glimpse of yet another long-enduring Jewish cultural type, the *maskil*, the scholarly learned man, the figure who hovers in the background of all of Perelman's work, too. After all, to find one's Kantian *"Critique of Metaphysical Reality"* compared to a paperback bestseller is only humorous to the extent that one assumes a higher aspiration to one's writing than the bestseller lists and a big movie sale. Speaking of Jewish writers in *Freud, Jews and Other Germans*, Peter Gay notes that "for centuries, Jews had needed literacy for their prayers even more than for their business, and the road to prestige at home or in the community led through scholarship, or at least verbal facility."[40] Just as with Perelman, Woody Allen's burlesque derives in part from the application of an elevated vocabulary and aesthetics to subjects unworthy of them, one symptom of "intellectual" comedy. Sanford Pinsker noticed Perelman's effect on Allen's prose, and said that if *"influence* may be too strong a term, there is no question about admiration. Woody Allen freely admits it."[41] Both are of course anti-authoritarian comics (most comedy is anti-authoritarian), but both have seemed to shy away from the larger political targets—their prey is more likely to be a pretentious intellectual or a flatulent novelist than a person with real power in the world. And if Pinsker is correct in identifying their favorite hate-objects as one of America's "self-appointed czars of the intellect," both Allen and Perelman are also alike in their preference for bookish and playful exercises rather than in hitching humor to a serious moral subject. Philip Roth once showed his distaste for the moralistic and sentimental strain of Jewish-American humor by saying this of Harry Golden's *For 2¢ Plain, Only in America*, and *Enjoy, Enjoy*: "Garnished with a little Manichewitz horseradish, the perplexed banalities of the middle class come back to [the reader] as the wisdom of the ages."[42] Few writers could be more self-consciously aware of the pitfalls of a sentimentally "Jewish" approach than Perelman and Allen, and few more conscientious in avoiding the "perplexed banalities" of ethnic gush. Both claim citizenship in the larger world of comic letters, neither styles himself a humorist of Jewish culture merely.

Arguing from the comparisons and connections we have drawn to other Jewish comic artists, then, it seems possible to claim that Perelman is, finally, a figure who can be interpreted in light of a special cultural tradition, although his case seems at first glance out of the ordinary. Certainly a historian of Jewish culture like Irving Howe finds Perelman outside the mainstream, even outside the principle variants of Jewish response to the New World and its possibilities: "Toward the pretensions of the world he adopted a strategy of ruthless deflation, something common enough to satirists, but here taken a step further, toward a demolition of the idea of order itself. . . . [Perelman became] a master of canny inconsequence, wild puns, and the stolid parodying of clichés."[43]

Perhaps Howe finds Perelman's comedy hard to classify because it is, on the surface, neither ethnic nor political, both modes we have come to associate with the idea of a specifically Jewish comedy. But to scratch that surface of "inconsequence" seems to me to reveal a real Jewishness underneath. Thus, from the Yiddish theatrical tradition we might find a residue of vitality and clownishness in Perelman's prose, and from Jewish comedians (professional or streetcorner) the

free-form energy of the *shpritz*. All comedy attempts to reduce its
subject, and the alliance of Jews with comedy itself (perhaps so
overfamiliar to us that we take it for granted) is perhaps best explained
if we recall that the uses of power were almost always *against* the
Jews: comedy is a defense, or, more accurately, a counteroffensive,
and Perelman's comedy, however playful it appears, is indeed something of a militant act. We can also agree that few cultures are as
literary or as scholarly as the Jewish, and, although in parody form,
Perelman's work is literary and scholarly to a rare degree: one can
only cite it as an unofficial impression, but his reputation and
popularity in graduate schools, English departments, publishing
circles, public broadcasting facilities, book reviews, and other venues
of the humanities establishment seems higher than that of any other
literary humorist, even now rivaled only by Perelman's self-confessed
disciple, Woody Allen. Further, Perelman's lifelong concern with the
defacement of words and works of literature, with the betrayal of high
art by charlatans, is a particularly Jewish sort of response; guardians of
a five-thousand-year-old moral and literary heritage, Jewish culture is
partially defined by its ready assumption of the responsibility of this
sort of custodianship, and it is not hard to understand how an impulse
toward parody and satire might arise from that self-imposed obligation: those forms of comedy are a means of striking back. Burlesque,
parody, satire, and literary imitation in general are also literary
stategies that allow a writer to appropriate the vital energy of the
popular arts while still preserving an air of ironic disapproval, and
there exist simultaneously in Perelman (just as in the Yiddish theater)
an exuberance with borrowed costumes coupled with an aspiration
toward higher things. In his pieces, however, these are, of course,
underlit with a sophisticated sense of irony. More than with any other
form, parody allows an imagination to have its cake and eat it, and
Perelman's deepest secret is that he always realized this.

"I'm a great believer in tradition," Perelman told one reviewer.
"None of us springs full blown from the head of Zeus. We're all part
of the flow of the river of life. If you know the past you can fit in and
flow along with the river."[44] Perhaps if he were one or two generations
younger, Perelman's humor would have been even more specifically
"traditional," even more overtly Jewish in its subject matter. But in

1904 Perelman was born into a very different America than the one we
see about us now, for at present we seem to be a country entering into
late middle age with an impoverished (and largely irrelevant) frontier
legacy more or less exhausted and showing every evidence that infalli-
ble symptom of cultural fatigue, nostalgia. For the first time in
America's history, the past seems preferable to the future. But in
1904, America looked only to the future, and as the son of immigrants, Perelman must have been mightily affected by those promised
possibilities of dignified assimilation offered up so unreservedly in our
national ethic. It is only from our vantage point in time and experience that we can see that much might have been lost in the hurry to
make oneself over into an unhyphenated American, in refusing to
exploit one's cultural legacy in the interests of a career. Still, one
wonders if Perelman will not finally prove to have exercised the larger
wisdom by insisting on his right to be regarded as a man of letters
among other men of letters, not as the special advocate and recording
angel of a transient subculture. After all, his friends called him "Sid,"
but on the printed page it was "S. J."—an Anglophile affectation that
perhaps tells us a little more about the writer than he would have liked
to admit, but one clue to a defense against the parochial and ethnic
that may finally prove to be the wiser choice. Although he claimed
that he did not expect his reputation to "outlast Mount Rushmore,"
all writers worth discussing write for the future as well as for the
present, and Perelman's refusal to overspecialize himself is the best
defense against those two grim old loan-sharks, Time and Fashion.

Chapter Five
The Perelman Technique
Travel

Speaking roughly, there are four points of departure for Perelman's comic flights in prose: (1) most often other people's writing, whether *Ulysses*, Jules Verne, *Tarzan of the Apes*, an advertising fatuity in *Vogue*, or a Schrafft's menu; (2) the show-biz scene; (3) the routine terrors of owning a home and the land it stands upon, and the comic possibilities inherent in the world of maids, cooks, hired hands, domestic animals, plumbing, and visiting relatives; and (4) travel.

Travel provided Perelman with the simplest comic springboard, and his persona in these pieces is that classic figure of fun, the innocent abroad, a bedeviled narrator who finds himself a victim who can revenge himself only with words. All writers inherit a tradition; good ones perfect it. It is no exaggeration to say that Perelman perfected the comic travel piece, once and for all. And if his formula is changeless and stylized as a Chaplin two-reeler, it is no less a model of the type.

"I really do love to travel," Perelman told Roy Newquist, "and I find, as far as copy is concerned, that the stresses and strains one encounters with customs officials and hotel capers and all that sort of thing is highly productive of the kind of situation I can write about." Although Perelman speaks only for himself, we might even hypothesize that travel is in its essence one of the richest mines of all for a writer of the comic persuasion. Smollett, Swift, Dr. Johnson, Lewis Carroll, Mark Twain, Jules Verne, Evelyn Waugh, and Vladimir Nabokov have all found travel, real or imaginary, peculiarly suited to their genius and created out of its juxtapositions and contrasts some of the most entertaining comic prose in our language.

For Perelman's purposes, travel not only creates difficulties and contretemps that are comic, but offers him the opportunity of reporting for us the chemical reduction of his own romantic expectations in the universal solvent of observed reality: "from bar mitzvah on," he informs us, "I had longed to qualify as a Jewish Robert Louis Stevenson." Thus, the wry humor in his travel writing is created out of the poignant contrast between an N. C. Wyeth—illustrated *Treasure Island* read under the covers by flashlight and the very humdrum locales a grown-up Perelman will discover lying in wait to disappoint him behind the very romantic Technicolor versions of some place names. In every case, the aesthetic distance between boyhood illusion and adult fact is about the same as from a Wagner overture to a dial-tone. But once again, his loss is our gain.

From typhoid shot through the home-movie recapitulation eight months later, Perelman mines a 1947 around-the-world junket with cartoonist and caricaturist Al Hirschfeld for every laugh he can get—and also manages to include some very pungent and admirable straight reporting, as well. *Westward Ha! or, Around the World in Eighty Clichés*, takes us first to the Chinese port of Chinwangtao, then on to Shanghai, Hong Kong and Macao, Singapore and the Malay states, Siam, India, Egypt, Naples, Nice, Paris, and finally London before coming back to New York: bankrolled by *Holiday* magazine, Perelman and Hirschfeld were going to do the whole Crayon box, and they started on a tramp steamer right out of Jack London, too. But of course reality always has a way of intruding.

In 1947, China was succumbing to the Communist revolution which immediately followed the war, and Chinwangtao was an impoverished industrial port "reminiscent of the less attractive suburbs of Carteret, New Jersey" (M, 363). Hong Kong recalls Asbury Park out of season to Perelman, and Bombay's Victorian architecture puts him in mind of "a third-rate Ohio university." Perelman makes a side trip from Chinwangtao to see the Great Wall of China, but tells us that "the Great Wall can also be seen facing page 556 of the *Encyclopedia Britannica* by simply stretching your hand toward the bookcase, though the chances of picking up a flea are very much smaller," and Shanghai, despite its fabled reputation, is all fake-ivory backscratchers and ashtrays of bogus cloisonné. When our two homespun American boys get a chance to meet honest-to-God Eastern royalty, the prince regent of the Malay state of Johore is impatient to learn from ex-

Hollywood screenwriter Perelman if Greer Garson really wears falsies. The "gambling hell" of Macao contains no "lovely, haggard women staking their last franc on the turn of a card," nor a single "lean, satanic" operator with a monocle and evening clothes straight out of the pages of spy novelist E. Phillips Oppenheim—in fact, the gambling hell of Macao turns out to be an infernal region of quite another kind: "a bleak, echoing auditorium of the type favored by Lithuanian glee clubs for their monthly singfests"(*M*, 344). A Malaysian rubber plantation is nothing more than a vast inland sea of rubber trees and "unless your name is Harvey Firestone, it is doubtful if the sight of twelve thousand acres of future hot-water bottles will affect you as the Grecian urn did Keats" (*M*, 350). The night life of Bombay conjures up that of "Schwenksville, Pennsylvania," and of all the "lethargic, benighted, somnolent fleabags this side of Hollywood, the port of Georgetown on the island of Penang is the most abysmal" (*M*, 356). The food is usually terrible everywhere they dock, and sometimes Perelman even gets to see it again; enduring a spell of very dirty weather in the Indian Ocean, Perelman renders the experience of seasickness with lyrical precision: "Liver and colon, lung and lights, all the shiny interior plumbing I had amassed so painstakingly in dribs and drabs over the years, fused into a single hard knot and wedged in my epiglottis"(*M*, 369). Every cabman, waiter, and bellhop is out to gouge the tourist, every meal east of Suez is an act of masochism (my favorite item is "a dab of penicillin posing as a potato"), and the temperature always seems to be in three figures— climaxing with a nice, round 119°F. at the Sphinx, where the brain-boiling heat is accompanied with a living cloud of sand-flies and the vista is defiled by the presence of a soda-pop stand.

These are Perelman's stock traveling gags, of course, and they are very funny. But there is more here than comic squalor; there is humanity, beauty, and numerous touches of fine descriptive prose. Reviewing the volume for the *New York Times*, Eudora Welty complains that "it would have been nice to have our Perelman straight, not constricted by a job to fulfill." In fact, it seems to me that Perelman's work for *Holiday* and the reportorial obligations that the journey imposed allow him to exhibit a more sober and eloquent facet of his talent than we usually get to see.

For example, the freighter *Marine Flyer* contains a cargo worth about a million and a half dollars, and Perelman is fascinated with the details of that "terrifying hash stored up by some insane magpie"(*M*, 330); he itemizes no fewer than thirty-five kinds of things aboard, from bulldozers through depilatories, from phonograph records through eleven barrels of ginger rejected by American restaurantgoers and on the way back to Hong Kong. As a *memento mori*, Perelman points out that "in Number 3 hatch admidships lay two Chinese cadavers, snugly flanked by mouthwash, desk calendars, insect bombs, and movie film." The effect of the passage is then not that of a quick riffle through the pages of a Sears catalog, but of a chaperoned tour of a private and eccentric museum, and our interest is engaged by Perelman's appeal to that queer human fascination with detail and contrast. For example, he tells us that there are a hundred and sixty cases (no more, no less) of Portuguese brandy on their way to the United States consulates in the East, and this off-hand detail tells us something in passing about those consulates and the American mission abroad that we might clumsily paraphrase with terms like "self-indulgent," "expensive," "phony," "anxious to impress." On the banks of the Ganges, Perelman and Hirschfeld are shown what should be a grave and impressive sight, the ashes of the recently cremated Hindu dead; but Perelman recovers psychological reality for us by pointing out that, far from awing the mind with the transience of life and impressing on it the somber finality of our organic destiny, these mounds of ash "had no real significance," and that the effect was in fact entirely negligible: "in the fierce glare of midday, on this eroded riverbank, the impact of the dissolution of the flesh was as paltry as a Boy Scout wienie roast" (*M*, 366).

In almost every instance, Perelman's prose deftly particularizes the *feel* of a place. For example, the travelers were relieved to discover that they loved the Taj Mahal despite all the "ecstatic nonsense" gushed up in its honor over the centuries, and Perelman particularizes it with an effective image: "the fragile delicacy of a soap bubble."

Reminders of the Vichy disgrace coupled with Nazi occupation reduced their stay in Paris to a few days, and "the lengthy visit we had projected soon shrank to the dimension of a condolence call." An Italian mountain village is caught once and for all with this prose snapshot: "At Viterbo, a somnolent mountain hamlet out of a Shubert operetta, we dallied long enough to gulp down a flask of memorable white wine and allow a bullock to trample on my foot," and the yokel's experience of the Monte Carlo gambling casino is described with a dexterity in three or four comic concise flashes: "a fiendish wooden rake darting at me like an adder and decimating my stack of counters; a vinegary cashier with the face of a bluebottle fly spurning my wristwatch as if it were infected; a short interregnum of Greco-Roman wresting with a doorman; and the springy recoil of a privet hedge as I soared over a white marble balustrade and bounced into it" (*M*, 384). Perelman even parodies himself in his *Monkey Business* days by claiming his rapid series of captions are "technically akin to what are termed Vorkapich shots in Hollywood." A cartoon to be sure, but a cartoon drawn with great verve and craftsmanship. Perelman, like his companion Hirschfeld, is a first-rate caricaturist.

One of Perelman's last, best discoveries on the journey was that of the English comedienne Hermione Gingold, whose style he describes as "an amalgam of Groucho Marx and Tallulah Bankhead," and it is pleasant for the reader returning now to the book to discover its anticipation that Gingold would prance to the Pantages stage on American television ten years later to accept Perelman's Oscar for him at the Academy Awards presentations when he refused to return to Hollywood and endure the "bourgeois babble" surrounding the Academy's annual orgy of self-congratulation.

Swiss Family, Farm Family

Perelman once said that the comic writer always works under the threat that his "invitation to perform is liable to wear out any moment," and that of all the kinds of writing a literary artist can undertake, comedy is perhaps the most difficult for a writer to sustain: "he must quickly and constantly amuse in a short span, and the first smothered yawn is a signal to get lost." In his travel writing Perelman is perhaps less oppressed by such demands than usual, and it is here that we find a more expansive, less hectic comic writer than in any of the other forms and formulae he adopts. Perelman was to go back to the travel format again and again.

In 1950 *The Swiss Family Perelman* appeared, a collection of twelve pieces detailing something of the same global itinerary we found in

Westward Ha!: a sojourn through Micronesia and the Malay peninsula, then on to Hong Kong and Europe. *Holiday* was again the sponsor and Hirschfeld again the illustrator, but this time Perelman was accompanied by his wife and children—Adam was twelve, Abbey ten. He would have taken the suggestion as an insult, but *The Swiss Family Perelman* is the only extended work of Perelman's that would serve as a situation for television situation comedy—and not a half bad one, at that. As with every sitcom, there is an inexhaustible source of plot energy: here, good old American folk set down amid the fascinating eccentricities of the exotic East. When they make it into a television series, Abbey must be made to practice her cello, even while she pines for chicken enchiladas; Adam can have freckles and a monkey always doing funny monkey things; and both kids can get everyone in scrapes when they learn to change money on the Hong Kong black market or take a lovable orphan (who is of course only pretending to be an orphan) under their wing.

The kids cannot be allowed to forget their schoolwork, and the elders must be suborned into teaching them all about that "unattractive dullard named Farmer Brown who [has] cut up his lower forty into rhomboids or isosceles triangles and [is] unable to compute the square of the hypotenuse."[5] If a higher quotient of danger or patriotic boilerplate is deemed necessary to hype the Neilsen ratings, a Communist-inspired uprising and a few plastique satchel-charges in theater lobbies can be introduced now and again. The Oriental servants can be won over to American ways, or misinterpret them with sorceror's-apprentice consequences. Relatives can visit. The Perelmans have rented out a Manhattan apartment and a Pennsylvania farm back in the states, and all kinds of things can go haywire there. In every case, the twain shall be made to meet.

Of course the undercurrent of disillusion that Perelman's narrational voice always introduces would have to be eliminated; a weekly media series cannot be expected to create good clean fun for thirty million viewers if it includes in its substance those grim coffin-nails of perception by which Perelman secures his comic prose to psychological reality, e.g., even in the tropical paradise of Bali we must come fact to fact with the ultimate blasphemy television will never be allowed to present: boredom. "The chilling truth, however, was that when you had seen one cremation, one tooth-filling ceremony, and one cockfight, you had seen them all."[6]

The Swiss Family Perelman is one of Perelman's finest collections, even funnier than *Westward Ha!* because its central situation is more conducive to comic by-play. The reviews were lovely. For example, Lee Rogow of the *Saturday Review of Literature* sounded that note of startled admiration and envy that professional writers so frequently emit when they comment on Perelman: "I must say that the Master's English, which he himself appears to have invented, is one of the diadems of our tribal *sprach*," he said, and went on to compare its delicious voluptuousness with "the showcase at Barney Greengrass' delicatessen"[7]—high praise indeed! A writer who is not flattered by being compared to a deli showcase is no writer at all.

Not that Perelman had to go out East with the whole cast of Perelmans demonstrates his nonpareil delicatessen delights, either. His 1947 collection *Acres and Pains* was justly hailed by Richardson Wright in the *New York Herald-Tribune Book Review* "as the funniest book of all on country living,"[8] and it is hard to do anything but agree. Although each and every situation, stage-prop, and caricature is absolutely predictable—Perelman puffing himself up as a country squire, the little woman always yearning for the city or rousing him out of a hammock to repair the roof, the neighboring yokels a pack of scheming country slickers—the twenty short pieces in *Acres and Pains* are the genre miniatures of a master, and if they are indeed traditional exercises, they are exercises so perfectly done as to achieve a sort of textbook finality. Richard Maloney of the *Times* put it best when he pointed out that Perelman worked with clichés, but clichés run through "backwards, as witches do the Lord's Prayer," and that the "fabulous virtuosity" of Perelman's language leaves the reader with a "pleasant daze similar to that experienced by users of cocaine. He is a stylist whose style is absolutely indescribable."[9]

Termites in the foundation, the well-pump breaking down, poison sumac the only thriving vegetation, remodeling performed by cretins who abscond even before your checkbook has "hardly ceased thrashing about in its final agony," maids that condescend to their employers and cows that eat a special feed weighed out on jewelers' scales, general store proprietors who rub oil of Shylock on their palms whenever they see Perelman approaching—the cast and plot of *Acres and Pains* have the changelessness of a passion play, and although Alan Brien reports that "in softer moments, glancing around as if fearful of being overheard in an obscenity," Perelman admitted that something in him responded to "hearing the grass grow,"[10] the prose epistles he sets before us are obviously only cartoons. These cartoons appear in series, and their essence is a continuing one: "at its core stands the shabby-genteel spokesman of these lines, slowly shedding his sanity as a terrifying vortex of dogs, debts and petty afflictions swirls sluggishly about his knees." From *Mr. Blandings Builds His Dreamhouse* through television's "Green Acres," the mechanism of naive and incompetent city mouse amid the vexations of the countryside deserves a code number and an entry all to itself in *The Reader's Handbook*; but of all the writers who have tried their hand at it, Perelman's use of country living as a comic motif is surely among the most skillful, irascible, and fun to reread.

Cloudland Revisited

But if travel and the country home offered obvious targets for Perelman's comedy, his most distinctive efforts have always been more literary in origin. Of all the hundreds of pieces Perelman has written using someone else's prose as a springboard, none surpass the series he called "Cloudland Revisited" for sheer comic delightfulness, and although after twenty-two of them Perelman came to feel he had exhausted the device, the "Cloudland" pieces constitute some of the finest comic writing in our heritage. As autobiography, they allow us a keyhole Perelman that is, like any keyhole glimpse, narrow but fascinating. As art, they are, like so many brilliant inventions, at once so inevitable as to seem startlingly fresh. Perelman simply reads again or sees again a book or movie that had thrilled him when he was young. Obviously, the experience is not the same. No one could believe otherwise. The moths of time, indifference, and disillusion will have gotten into the magic carpet of childhood's ability to believe, and the return to the thrill will inevitably be saturated with anticlimax and melancholy. Speaking of his rereading of George Barr McCutcheon's *Graustark*, for example, Perelman notes rather poignantly that "our reunion, like most, left something to be desired,"[11] and we might use that comment as a caption for each and every

"Cloudland" piece. But of course this unrequited longing to reenter the past is not in itself the stuff of comedy, and it is really Perelman's witty and acerbic commentary on the work he is revisting that gives each piece its charm.

It is also important to see that this frame of ironic commentary is not just simple mockery, either, although Perelman sometimes pretends that it is. We are enchanted in part because Perelman's wit and intelligence, his imaginative energy, manage to evoke in us a sort of campy participative exhilaration, a touch of the original adolescent thrill itself. Good comic writing frequently creates a sort of perverse affection for its objects, no matter how vehement its rhetorical disapproval of those objects may be, and in the "Cloudland" pieces we experience once more a little of what it felt like when we discovered Jules Verne, Edgar Rice Burroughs, or Sax Rohmer for the first time, but with our return now poignantly shadowed by a valedictory sense of seeing from the outside those excitements that can be experienced from the inside only once. Even if the gremlins of experience and sheer living (always something of a disappointment) have gotten at the book or movie, "curdled the motivation, converted the hero into an insufferable jackanapes, drawn mustaches on the ladies . . . and generally sprinkled sneeze powder over the derring-do,"[12] Perelman demonstrates that there is a little wobbly flight still left in the old magic carpet even if it takes a comic incantation to conjure it out.

Perelman was always something of a dandy, and if the opening paragraphs of his "Cloudland" pieces do not creak with *Sturm and Drang* about his adolescent Oedipal situation, they do indeed supply us with some fascinating footnotes to American social history. And even if Perelman's memories are not focused on an era most of us are old enough to remember, we are still glad to see such a capable mind on duty to do the remembering. Few human acts are so universally pleasant to observe as the act of recall, no matter what the object, no matter how obscure or peculiar or trivial the detail. To conjure up a bit of the past is always to recover for a moment something precious from that universal solvent of time and indifference and superfluousness in which almost everything is eventually dissolved, and Perelman is a master at such minor alchemy. At the dawn of the Jazz Age, Perelman assures us, he was a young blood who wanted to appear as sophisticated as Wallace Reid, and to this end he dressed for soirées in a wasp-waisted tweed suit with a yellow bow tie to set it off, and did the tango or the toddle or the balçonade to *La Veeda, Dardanella*, or *Wildflower*. His trousers were of unbleached sisal, and had twenty-two-inch bottoms, as in a John Held, Jr., cartoon. He tells us that as a blade in good standing he smoked straw-tipped Melachrinos and gave the girls chocolate creams, and he recalled that the bands had names like Coon-Sanders and his Blackhawk Orchestra or the Mound City Blue Blowers. A metal hip-flask filled with gin warmed to 98.6° was of course an obligatory male appurtenance, and the stylish female hair style of the era included big curls called "cootie garages." "Wave on wave of such Proustian memories—well, if not waves, a needle shower"[13] always precede Perelman's departure back into the past. Since Jules Verne's creations have exerted a lifelong spell on Perelman, a "Cloudland Revisited" piece called "Roll On, Thou Deep and Dark Scenario, Roll" seems a good example of cloudland with which to begin looking at his approach.

The year is 1916, and although in the very first sentence we are reminded that there is an immense war being fought in Europe, here at Narragansett Bay a much smaller and less destructive fantasy is going to be acted out: Sidney Perelman, age twelve, is attempting to play the part of Captain Nemo from *Twenty Thousand Leagues Under the Sea*.

There must be a few American males who never tried to be deep-sea divers with homemade equipment, but Perelman is really attempting only his own personal version of a boyhood fantasy millions have essayed with no better results. One can only smile ruefully in recognition: boots filled with scrap-iron ballast and a bicycle pump linked to a garden hose for oxygen. The helmet is of course the crucial element of hardware, and Perelman has improvised his from a metal lard pail. His choice of air-breathing, air-pumping assistant is equally unfortunate, too, for Perelman has to make do with an irascible and incompetent youth he calls "Piggy Westervelt," and when Perelman submerges himself and the leaky hose starts pumping water into the lard-pail helmet, only the timely intervention of a Portuguese eel fisherman in a rowboat saves him. The boys had been scouting for Blackbeard's bullion and plate, or at least one of those lumps of ambergris alert Horatio Alger newsboys were always cashing in for forty thousand dollars, but Perelman's literary recycling of the episode was perhaps its only worthwhile by-product—and even that recycling comes some thirty-five years after the event. The whole experience was in fact so depressing that Perelman tells us that "for years I never mentioned the ocean floor save with a sneer." But the eel fisherman had correctly identified Perelman's escapade as the sincerest form of flattery: "'Who the hell do you think you are?' he demanded, outraged, 'Captain Nemo?'" Here indeed was the point of intersection between art and life, for a movie version of Verne's subaqueous classic was showing locally in 1916, and *everyone* had seen it. And so it is to this "Cloudland" that Perelman returns in 1952, courtesy of the Museum of Modern Art film library. Lo and behold, the film one remembers hardly resembles the film on the screen: "like most sentimental excursions into the past, [my return] was faintly tinged with dissillusion."

Three Verne novels had been pureed into the 1916 silent, along with "a sanguinary tale of betrayal and murder in a native Indian state that must have fallen into the developing fluid by mistake" (*M*, 573). Perelman takes a backhand swipe at the arty subculture of *cinéastes* even as he prepares a lengthy indictment (and an even longer rope) for the film's director, Stuart Paton, whose alchemical powers of transmuting straightforward adventure into murky melodrama he finds astonishing: "I daresay that if [he] were functioning today, the votaries of the Surrealist film who sibilate around the Little Carnegie and the Fifth Avenue Playhouse would be weaving garlands for his hair. That man could make a cryptogram out of Mother Goose." Notice in passing Perelman's casually authoritative accuracy in the use of movie-house sociology. Like any good district attorney he names names.

In a review of Perelman's work, Paul Theroux uses the image of air piracy to give us a memorable metaphor for a humorist in full attack: "In a sense, the humorist is like the man who hijacks a jumbo jet and its 300 passengers by threatening the pilot with a 10-cent water pistol. The arsenal is simple—technique matters, manner is everything, and fury helps."[14] With a quick précis of the movie's flapdoodle, Perelman not only fills us in on its plagiarisms and pretensions but manages to make the film's ridiculousness charmingly patent. "Nemo is Melville's Captain Ahab with French dressing, as bizarre a mariner as ever trod on a weevil," and the wonders of the deep as viewed through the portholes of the *Nautilus* "approximate what anybody might see who has quaffed too much sacramental wine and is peering into a home aquarium." Perelman's four paragraphs of plot summary emphasize outraged common sense, and his most effective technique is the seemingly casual aside. For example, Paton has spliced several impenetrable subplots into the narrative out of sheer directorial whim. One of these subplots features a retired ocean trader (nowhere mentioned by the "great romancer" Verne, Perelman loyally assures us) who is haunted by the avenging phantasms of a Indian maharani he had caused to commit suicide, including "by the way, a rather engaging Mephistopheles of the sort depicted in advertisements for quick-drying varnish." That ten-cent water pistol is being wielded by a master.

The picture flounders to a conclusion, all coincidence and bubbles, but the denouement at least includes a scene of "authentic grisly charm" when the surviving mariners bury Nemo at the bottom of the sea, "pettishly tossing the coffin into a clump of sea anemones." Just as with all the other revisits he makes for his twenty-two "Cloudland" pieces, Perelman discovers in the "erstwhile jaunty narrative [has] developed countless crow's-feet and wrinkles"(*M*, 481).

"Crow's-feet and wrinkles" have also come to disfigure the resurrected visage of *The Mystery of Dr. Fu-Manchu*, but a least that famous melodrama offers Perelman one of his finest comic opportunities. Sax Rohmer (the pen name of Arthur Sarsfield Wade) began publishing his accounts of "the most malign and formidable" evil genius in the annals of American subliterature just before World War I, an era characterized by a degree of racial chauvinism in the American public arts that can startle and embarrass us today. "The cruel cunning of an entire Eastern race" is one of Rohmer's favorite adjective clusters to describe Dr. Fu-Manchu's malignity, and the Mephistophelian creature is again and again characterized as "the yellow peril incarnate in one man," an apocalyptic threat to "the entire white race." And of course Rohmer's plot contrivances are irresistibly silly, especially after Perelman's wit has had its flattening way with them. Thus, after the malign doctor's assistant, Kâramanéh, saves our British detectives from drowning in the Thames by extending to them her false pigtale, Perelman caps his summary of the incident with this drollery: "It is at approximately this juncture that one begins to appreciate how lightly the laws of probability weighed on Sax Rohmer. Once you step with him into Never-Never Land, the grave's the limit, and no character is deemed extinct until you can use his skull as a paper-weight" (*M*, 458–59).

Technically, the mode and tone here is what is classified as "Horatian satire"; the speaker's persona is urbane, witty, and tolerantly amused by the child's play he sees enacted down there beneath his elevated and quasi-aristocratic vantage point. There is a negligible amount of passion or indignation (compare, say, Swift's underlying fury and disgust in "A Modest Proposal," which would be classified as "Juvenalian satire"). The tone in Perelman's piece is relaxed, gentlemanly, playful, cosmopolitan. Social and moral correction are not being advocated; in fact, nothing strenuous or serious is even remotely at issue. Almost all of Perelman's work is of this mode, and it might also be emphasized that the reader is implicitly flattered to be included in the disdainful irony of the tone. It is, essentially, a courtly tone, the wave-length of a privileged minority. This last point, central to our appreciation of Perelman, can be made clearer by contrast if we call to mind the manner in which we connect with the narrative voice in *Huckleberry Finn*, or in James Thurber's "You Could Look It Up," or with Holden Caulfield's voice in *The Catcher in the Rye*. In these instances the creator and the reader wink conspiratorially at each other over the heads of the narrators, above the level of discourse established by the narrative persona, for the writer and reader are a bit more sophisticated and aware than the narrator mediating between them. Thus, Holden Caulfield serves as his creator's mouthpiece in almost every issue from artistic integrity to the spirit of social egalitarianism; but we also laugh *at* Holden, for Holden is not quite aware enough to realize that Salinger is sharing a laugh with us at his expense. Here Holden speaks to the adorable, bitchy Sally Hayes with unpolished and admirable sincerity, but even if we agree with his position intellectually and emotionally, we are implicitly invited to laugh *at* him, too:

"Take cars," I said it in this very quiet voice. "Take most people, they're crazy about cars. They worry if they get a little scratch on them, and they're always talking about how many miles they get to a gallon, and if they get a brand-new car already they start thinking about trading it in for one that's even newer. I don't even like *old* cars. I mean they don't even interest me. I'd rather have a goddam horse. A horse is at least *human*, for God's sake."[15]

Not that Perelman cannot arrange to have a narrator indict himself out of his own mouth; as his neglected play *The Beauty Part* reveals, he can be what has come to be called "indirect satire"—allowing the characters to make themselves ridiculous. But in his more characteristic prose pieces (and any or all of the "Cloudland" episodes would qualify here), Perelman works just inside the flimsy pasteboard partitions that mark off literary burlesque and travesty from the other fiefdoms and demesnes of the kingdom of the comic. Although the term "burlesque" has of course come to connote middle-age stripteasers in Schubert hippodromes and comedians with ties that light up, the term originally indicated an imitation of a serious literary work that creates amusement out of the disparity between the high style and the low subject matter, or vice versa: that is, the real butt of the exercise is likely to be the literary work being imitated and ridiculed, not the manners and morals of society or man's inhumanity to man. Literary style, not human nature, is frequently the object being brought forward for chastisement and correction.

We might also notice once again that the parody offers us a chance for some "forbidden" fun while allowing us to preserve our intellectual dignity, too, no small part of its attraction. For his burlesque here, Perelman's method is not to simply make a few sarcastic remarks about Sax Rohmer's clumsiness; instead, he himself enters into the spirit of the fun by using exaggeration of fact and vocabulary to explode the pretensions of his target. Nor does the explosion merely destroy, deflate: it also releases energy and creates momentum. Thus, Perelman tells us that when he was twelve years old he came across a book that "exerted a considerable influence on my bedtime habits." Of course the reader is alerted to the fact that S. J. Perelman, being S. J. Perelman, cannot just leave the claim at that: the technique of fantastic exaggeration is almost always central to his comic method, and Rohmer's melodrama, one of the noisiest engines of purple prose ever assembled between the covers of a book, gives Perelman the perfect opportunity to work up some absurdities of his own:

Up to [the discovery of Dr. Fu-Manchu], I had slept in a normal twelve-year-old fashion, with the lights full on, a blanket muffling my head from succubi and afreets, a chair wedged under the doorknob, and a complex network of strings festooned across the room in a way scientifically designed to entrap any trespasser, corporeal or not. On finishing the romance in question, however, I realized that the protection I had been relying on was woefully inadequate and that I had merely been crowding my luck. Every night thereafter, before retiring, I spent an extra half hour barricading the door with a chest of drawers, sprinkling tacks along the window sills, and strewing crumpled newspapers about the floor to warn me of approaching footsteps. As a minor precaution, I slept under the bed. . . . (M, 453)

"Succubi" are female demons fabled to have sexual intercourse with sleeping men and "afreets" are the evil monsters of Arabian myth. Both terms are exotic specimens, arcane, archaic, and esoteric. But both are displayed here in precisely the right context, and both flatter us with an appeal to our own discriminating taste and appreciative eye. After all, a humorist less literary (or less elitist, if you prefer) would simply have substituted the word "ghosts," or used some familiar vampire lore, to get the same point across. And if Perelman was simply interested in having fun with the idea of a twelve-year-old boy frightened by the spirit world, he could make his point without resorting to such a rarefied vocabulary, that famous instrument that E. B. White compared to "a Wurlitzer organ that has three decks, 50 stops, and a pride of pedals."[16] But, of course, Perelman is not just interested in having a little foxy grandpa fun with the young, for he is also having a little connoisseur's fun with this enormous word collection, too, and a little magic carpet fun with the book that once upon a time took him all the way to cloudland and can still lift us off the floor a couple of inches before we stop believing and allow it to settle back. I cannot help but feel that part of the pleasure of reading a vintage Perelman piece is the empathy we feel in participating in an imaginative act that combines the heady essences of flight, nostalgia, crafts-

manship, and snobbery all at once. It is in fact characteristic that
Perelman's supreme literary admiration is reserved for the most
technically sophisticated, verbally complex, and widely erudite literary intelligence of our century, James Joyce, and it is important to see
that Perelman has more in common with Joyce than their shared
affection for linguistic potpourri and references drawn from every
level of Western culture from Shakespeare all the way down through
the humblest plastic gadgets of tabloid journalism.

Joyce always thought of himself as a *comic* writer, and one of the
most painful effects on him created by the weird combination of
pornographic scandal and academic solemnity that surrounded *Ulysses*
during his lifetime was that everyone who swarmed over that work
seemed to be interested mainly in the salacious content of Molly
Bloom's soliloquy or in the subtle Homeric and transcultural under-
structure beneath the novel's surface, ignoring in their eagerness for
smut or pedantry the comic byplay in which Joyce took so much
justifiable pride. Comedy is hardly incidental to Joyce's masterpiece,
and Perelman, who told interviewers that he could still "choke up
with respect for Joyce," and regarded the great Irish stylist as beyond
all comparison as the finest *comic* writer in the English canon, was one
of the keenest appreciators of its extensive use of parody, multilingual
puns, rhetorical wit, literary reference, and surreal horseplay. If the
only reader who could do justice to Joyce was Joyce himself, Perelman
would be instantly recognizable to the great man as at least a service-
able second.

Paul Theroux, a great admirer of Perelman's, pointed out that he
thought that Perelman had at the very least earned for himself a
permanent post in the literary criticism industry by his creation of a
full-scale parody of Joyce and the Lilliputian explicators and elfin
ghouls who swarm over the Dublin that Joyce photographed, x-rayed,
weighed, measured, anatomized, animated, mythologized, mourned,
and embalmed, on June 16, 1904. Perelman's piece is called "Anna
Trivia Pluralized"—Anna Livia Plurabelle, at once an incarnation of
woman, river, Ireland, and mythic consciousness, is one of the
presences of *Finnegans Wake*—and Theroux notes that the smooth
execution of the comic essay demonstrates that "it is only a stone's
throw from the shenanigans of Joyce to the hijinks of Perelman." The

Perelman parody, Theroux maintains, is superb, and "if parody is the subtlest form of literary criticism, then a piece such as 'Anna Trivia Pluralized' in *Baby, It's Cold Inside* (1970) is all Perelman needs for his directorship in that large corporation known as Joyce Studies."[17]

Perelman's anecdote is an extremely sophisicated play on the credulity of American scholars "discovering" people who claim they know the real-life models for characters for *Ulysses*, and Perelman, who obviously knew all the minutiae to be found in works like Richard Ellmann's great biography of Joyce, introduced arcana into his tale, such as that of Joyce's brief management of the Volta movie theater on Mary Street, that only a true disciple of the novelist and curator of its minutiae could possibly deploy. Although the "Rhode Island kid" never forgot his own origins, we find all through his fifty years of work that those little signatures of homage one gifted writer will go out of his way to give to those he reveres as his betters. For example, Perelman used a casual reference to Blazes Boylan, Molly Bloom's manager in her singing career, as the very epitome of the coarse and yet vital male lover, as the *sine qua non* of rakehell masculinity in one piece;[18] in another, he had a cat mewing "Mrkgnao," a most peculiar cat-sound "she had obviously learned from reading *Ulysses*." Odds and ends out of T. S. Eliot's poetry also find their way into Perelman's comic pieces by way of tribute, too: for example, if one were to be drowned in the Mediterranean he would be "sacked out with Phlebas the Phoenician," the imaginary figure whose "Death by Water" forms the shortest and most evocative passage (part 4) of *The Waste Land*. And in particularizing a Parisian astrologer, the sensual charlatan Mlle Mouton, we find Perelman's cultural references piled on with a trowel and culminating in a reference to "Mr. Eliot's Grishkin,"[19] the rather sinister Russian Jewess of "pneumatic bust" and "feline smell" whose flesh is so much more appealing than the cold and abstract metaphysics of the philosophers in the 1919 lyric, "Whispers of Immortality."

Thus, Joyce and Eliot, perhaps the two most formidable reputations in English letters in this century, lend code-terms and reference points to Perelman, but Perelman's deadly accuracy for imitating the contours of English prose style hardly stopped with the masters. "Farewell, My Lovely Appetizer," one of Perelman's most famous pieces, might serve as a specimen illustration for his constant concern with technique. This "casual" is a straight parody of Raymond Chandler's famous detective story—indeed, Chandler himself was delighted with it—and the narrator's voice is here a strict comic impersonation rather than a series of comments delivered from the outside. Mimicry, not just irony, is part of the performance:

"I could go for you, sugar," I said slowly. Her face was veiled, watchful. I stared at her ears, liking the way they were joined to her head. There was something complete about them; you knew they were there for keeps. When you're a private eye, you want things to stay put. (M, 191-96)

Like any great caricaturist from Daumier to David Levine, Perelman reduced and intensified the salient features of his model until he had created an imitation that was at once exaggerated enough to be funny while remaining accurate enough to be recognized. "Veiled, watchful," catches the pseudo-poetic diction so much favored by the tough-guy detective novelists of the thirties, and the fusion of Bogartian insouciance in the anatomical assessment and yet with that assessment directed toward the *wrong* features is of course the kernel of the comic device. The mock-profound street-wisdom that rounds out the paragraph—"When you're a private eye, you want things to stay put"—is a miniature masterpiece of comic imitation: the private detective, weary of the sordid underside of it all, would indeed yearn for "things to stay put" (at least this is the literary convention); but that the "things" he would yearn for to "stay put" are his secretary's "ears" is, to speak pedantically, not quite what we expect. "The sudden transformation of a strained expectation into nothing," Immanuel Kant called humor, and later commentators like M. H. Abrams have amended and amplified that insight to a more accurate equation: "the sudden satisfaction of an expectation, but in a way we did not in the least expect."[20] It might be added that Perelman's parody is not merely a witty imitation of the modern detective tale, he has also gone to the trouble of constructing a little mystery plot and working out the solution for us. Thus, we not only find ourselves amused by the humorist's impressive powers of comic mimicry and impersonation (" 'My few friends call me Mike,' I said pleasantly. 'Mike,' she said, rolling the syllable on her tongue. 'I don't believe I've ever heard that name before. Irish?' "), we also follow the little mystery storyline, too, and discover a microplot not really much more preposterous than the nonsense we are asked to believe in while we are engaged in a standard lending-library whodunit.

A cast-iron convention of the private-eye genre is that first visit to his office by a beautiful and glamorous and very nervous woman, almost always a high-society figure, almost always giving us the impression that *her* version of the attempt on her life in the country club parking lot or the theft of those innocent-seeming deeds and her ex-husband's gutta percha hunting boots is not quite *all* the story. Lovers of the mystery yarn will have no trouble recognizing the cruel accuracy of Perelman's imitation:

"Suppose you take it from the beginning," I suggested.
  She drew a deep breath. "You've heard of the golden spintria of Hadrian?" I shook my head. "It's a tremendously valuable coin believed to have been given by the Emperor Hadrian to one of his proconsuls, Caius Vitellius. It disappeared about 150 A.D., and eventually passed into the possession of Hucbald the Fat. After the sack of Adrainople by the Turks, it was loaned by a man named Shapiro to the court physician, or hakim, of Abdul Mahmoud. Then it dropped out of sight for nearly five hundred years, until last August, when a dealer in secondhand books named Lloyd Thursday sold it to my husband."
  "And now it's gone again," I finished.
  "No," she said. "At least, it was lying on the dresser when I left, an hour ago. . . ."

The larger curve of this story of foolery is to create a comic thump as anticlimax is substituted for expectation. But the details are revealingly unique to Perelman. Notice the "after the sack of Adrianople by the Turks. . . ." This is erudition for erudition's sake, the simple love of scholarly minutiae on the part of a fact-lover. In his essay on Charles Dickens, George Orwell called a similar tell-tale detail in a passage of Dickens's "something totally unnecessary, a florid little squiggle on the edge of the page."[21] But Orwell did not condemn this baroque excess in Dickens's prose; far from it: "it is just by these squiggles that the special Dickens atmosphere is created." Perhaps

because we are accustomed to looking at literature almost exclusively
in terms of the larger issues it exhibits—its theme, its politics, its
stance toward sexuality and sex roles, its representation of historical
forces, its vision of the inevitable clash between society and individual—we are startled to find Orwell describing an important aspect of
a great writer's prose as a "squiggle." But a writer like Perelman must
be appreciated for his style—subtract the style and you lose the
essence of him—and the "special atmosphere" he creates with the use
of squiggles is central to his fascination. Nor are all of Perelman's
squiggles apparent; some of them are Joycean in their obscurity and
Nabokovian in their delicate naughtiness. The Chandler parody and
its use of "spintria" is a case in point.

After listing in his introduction to *Bend Sinister* the extremely
complicated and subtle manner in which he had written into his text a
web of micromotifs—erudite references, recurrent images, odds and
ends of popular culture altered for disparagement—Vladimir Nabokov gives the equivalent of a verbal shrug and says that, "It may be
asked if it is really worth an author's while to devise and distribute
these delicate markers whose very nature requires that they not be too
conspicuous."[22] The question is of course only rhetorical, for Nabokov, like any other constructor of puzzles, amuses himself mightily
by the deployment of these "delicate markers." All he really asks for is
a reader clever enough to be worthy of his game of hide and seek, for
there would be little pleasure in creating a labyrinth too easily solved,
enlisting too small a portion of one's powers of deception. Perelman,
like Nabokov and Joyce a lover of words and lover of games, has
painted into his Chandler parody a little *trompe l'oeil*, a squiggle that
only the bookish will care enough about to solve and appreciate. The
"spintria" his not-quite-innocent society dame speaks of is not a coin
at all, but a word so recondite that one can find it only in the Oxford
unabridged—"spintrian" pleasures pertain to "those who seek out, or
invent new and monstrous actions of lust." Since Perelman used the
good gray pages of the *New Yorker* circa 1944 for this blue joke, he has
disguised it so thoroughly only Scrabble players, crossword enthusiasts, or spintrians still in the closet would have noticed it, and the
rest of the magazine's readership would have taken the term at face
value, that is, as a synonym for "coin." Of course Perelman does not

have to conceal a double-entendre under his first meaning to create literary excitement, for this seems to me the rationale behind his famous vocabulary.

Where we expect the ordinary word or the common expression, we frequently receive from Perelman the arcane, the recondite, or the archaic. Thus, his vocabulary is part of his sheer invention. It adds something new, staves off the unexpected. A piece in Perelman's 1975 collection *Vinegar Puss* begins: "Of a wild and windy night this winter, any noctambule pausing to light his cheroot (or extinguish it; it comes to the same thing) outside a public house off Shaftesbury Avenue called the Haunch of Pastrami might have observed two individuals of no special distinction descending from an equipage before the premises."[23] and the piece goes on to parody Robert Louis Stevenson's *New Arabian Nights*.

Now a "noctambule" usually means a sleepwalker, a "somnambulist," who would consciously notice nothing at all in front of the Haunch of Salami; here of course Perelman simply means someone walking about at night. In fact, he might simply have said "someone walking about at night" and indicated the same thing by it, and been a good deal more readily understood in the bargain. But he chooses instead the arcane word, a word no one would ever use in normal discourse or prose. The reason he does so is to allow us to escape the iron confinement of the ordinary and the expected, and the appeal is to our intelligence and taste. It is an admirable intention and a charming gift, a scholar's passion for the rare with a craftsman's affection for the perfect fit.

Chapter Six
Resemblances
Ade and Benchley

"I consider myself purely traditional," Perelman told Roy Newquist, "a disciple of people like George Ade, Ring Lardner, Stephen Leacock, Robert Benchley, and Frank Sullivan. . . ."[1] He has also praised Dorothy Parker, whose taste and intelligence allowed her to keep her "standards very high."

Although almost unknown today, George Ade (1866–1944: a life begun the year after the Civil War ended and finished the year before Hiroshima), was an enormously popular and successful humorist around the turn of the century. His *Fables in Slang*, a compilation of newspaper columns originally written for the *Chicago Record*, was brought out in 1899 and sold an astonishing 70,000 copies. Obviously, Ade had struck the right chord. *More Fables in Slang* followed the next year, and the author and his publishers continued to exploit the device until, over the next three decades, Ade had put out 250 of the fables in ten volumes and, like Conan Doyle with his mind-child Sherlock Holmes, grown thoroughly sick and tired of the golden groove of self-repetition for profit.

Ade's pieces are neither real fables nor really told in slang: they are technically parables, for unlike the fairy-story components of true fables (which almost always endow animal characters with human attributes and magical energies), the parable is a simple tale stressing the analogy between its surface parts and a thesis or lesson that stands behind it, and need not depend on supernatural machinery to make its point. As for the style, the stories are not really couched in slang, but in the vernacular—that is, they are homey and colloquial but not vulgar or highly specialized in vocabulary; in fact, Ade eschewed using the "low discourse" of the racing track and the cant and code of thieves, insisting in a somewhat stuffy disclaimer that his pieces could

be "read with propriety in any family." Menchen called Ade "a boor
with a touch of genius," an unflattering and accurate description of
the author of the *Fables*, but a rereading of the pieces discloses the
qualities that might have attracted Perelman to them. Beneath a
genial surface, the parables reveal a core of sour dismay, and the target
they seek out almost obsessively is social or intellectual pretension.
"The Fable of the Good Fairy with the Lorgnette, and Why She Got It
Good" is a suitable illustration. The object of loathing in this parable
is the self-appointed lady bountiful, the smug and condescending
society matron who disguises her self-regard inside her good works:
"'Now, '" she announces, "'now to carry Sunshine into the Lowly
Places.'"

As soon as she struck the Plank Walks, and began stalking her prey, the
small Children would crawl under the Beds, while Mother would dry her
Arms on the Apron, and murmur, "Glory be!" They knew how to stand off
the Rent-Man and the Dog-Catcher; but when 235 pounds of Sunshine came
wafting up the Street, they felt that they were up against a New Game.[2]

Eventually a Scrappy Kid slings a tomato can at the Benevolent
Lady, and she gives up good works among the lower orders to devote
herself to an Ibsen club. As for the Scrappy Kid, "he grew up to be a
Corrupt Alderman, and gave his mother plenty of Good Clothes,
which she was always afraid to wear." Ade seems to be saying tacitly
that it is perhaps better to be a corrupt but happy politician (and one
who still remembers his mother, notice) than a used-up cipher lost in
the facelessness of the working class. Like every proper fabulist, Ade
sums up the point of his plot with an italicized moral; here it is *"In
uplifting, get underneath."* This epigrammatic wit is valid both on the
surface—physically, to lift "up," you do have to go "under"—and of
course as moral instruction: the "underneath" in society is animated
by actualities and motives and necessities that only the genteel can
afford to pretend do not exist. Ade, like Perelman, put realistic (and
thus equivocal) perceptions inside his wit, plain brown truths under
fancy wrappers, and he was on the whole not particularly impressed
with human nature—rather the reverse. I would guess it is this
underlying cynicism which allows Perelman to continue to be in-

trigued by him, and not the simple nostalgia offered by Ade's now-antique idiom or a craftsman's admiration for an era when they really knew how to make 'em: "Ade had a social sense of history," Perelman told William Zinsser. "His pictures of Hoosier life at the turn of the century are more documentary than any of those studies on how much people paid for their coal. His humor was rooted in a perception of people and places. He had a cutting edge and an acerbic wit. . . ."[3]

Since Jesse Bier's study of American comic writing is subtitled "The Rise and Fall of American Humor," we can confirm his premise of a declining legacy by noting that Ade's folksy parables eventually have their fangs removed and end up as the paper tigers purveyed by the "genial and harmless" Will Rogers, whose fake optimism and smarm Perelman loathed.

Mencken, Lardner, and Benchley present even more obvious similarities to Perelman's comic work than does Ade, and serve as the principal illustrations for that process by which we can retrospectively see the cosmopolitan satirists supersede the crackerbox wits, the city mice displace their country cousins, a quick, bold evolutionary acceleration that would bring American humor to its highest point during the decades between the wars, about 1920 to 1940.

Mencken's great and abiding enemy was the American spirit of puritanism (not coincidentally the spirit of the rural village where the crackerbox philosopher held forth), which he defined once and for all as "the haunting fear that someone, somewhere, may be happy." We have already seen how his *American Mercury* diatribes, part Savonarola and part smartaleck, exerted a "gravitational attraction" for young editors and writers like Perelman, who slavishly imitated the Mencken brimstone in the columns of schoolboy publications. In his flaying of "boobus Americanus," Mencken accused the frontier culture of the United States as pretending toward a phony piety like that of William Jennings Bryan and the prohibitionists, compounded with "a theology degraded almost to the level of voodooism." For Mencken, America before World War I was the benighted end-product of the "yokel's congenital and incurable hatred of the city man."[4]

Life repeating art, then, it is no accident that writers from the boondocks like Ring Lardner (of Niles, Michigan) first became newspaper writers for big-city journals, and then disillusioned, unhappy men in flight from Prohibition America and all that Prohibition represented. The most accurate portrait of Lardner in his ultimate self-befouling and self-destroying incarnation is that of the character of Abe North, the "entirely liquid" former songwriter who is eventually beaten to death in an argument in a New York club, in Fitzgerald's classic novel of the American expatriate experience and its consequences, *Tender Is the Night*. Perelman has expressed great admiration for Lardner's work: "at his best he was the nonpariel; nobody in America has ever equalled him."[5] In muted fashion, Perelman moved from small town to big city, too, and we have seen that Paris, "where the twentieth century was," exerted a spell on him as well.

Robert Benchley's life actually touched Perelman's at many points in their respective careers. Like Perelman, Benchley was an Ivy Leaguer (Harvard, class of 1912), and again like Perelman, he first began to make at least a campus name for himself as a cartoonist for the humor magazine, in Benchley's case the *Lampoon* (fellow editors who served with him on that most famous of all campus magazines were Frederick Lewis Allen, the social historian of the 1920s, and the *New Yorker* cartoonist Gluyas Williams). Perelman and Benchley were both *New Yorker* contributors from that magazine's early days under Harold Ross, and when Perelman's *The Best of S. J. Perelman* was published by Random House in 1947, it was entirely appropriate for Perelman to dedicate that volume, obviously his most important collection up to that date, to Robert C. Benchley. And Perelman has always been extremely generous in his praise of his colleague.

As we have already seen (in chapter 2), Benchley ended up as one of those "mouldering hulks" in the Hollywood Sargasso making Paramount movie shorts, but during the years when he still wrote comic prose he gave to our heritage some of its cleverest and most likable comic pieces. Again and again, Perelman has been linked with Benchley by anthologists. But if the verbal and referential sophistication we find in Benchley's things resembles that of Perelman more than a little, the atmosphere of Benchley's self-created world is quite different from his colleague's.

In their excellent survey, *America's Humor: from Poor Richard to*

Doonesbury, Walter Blair and Hamlin Hill described the Benchley persona as a gentle and incompetent suburban duffer set upon by forces from outside himself, and they show how Benchley always brings to his characterization the attributes of a classic Milquetoast: "the futility, the hopeless bravado, the glorious confusion, and the lurking terror."[6] In contrast, Perelman's comic alter ego is vastly more energetic, and not nearly as guiltless as Benchley's, and the respective worlds each of their protagonists moves through are not really alike. Perelman's world is a surreal cartoon, Benchley's only a slightly exaggerated version of our own. Blair and Hill make the point that "where the Benchley Little Man doggedly fights the real world in spite of unrelieved failure, the Perelman character is actually propelled into the world of fantasy."[7] In fact, it is not unfair to say that Benchley's writing might be described as a sort of comically tinted existentialism, sweet and sad but almost entirely empty and hopeless—Jean-Paul Sartre lightly coated with sugar, but despairing of the sheer dumb futility of mere 98.6° existence just the same.

Notice the sense of despair that lurks just beneath the surface of a piece Benchley calls "The Sunday Menace" and try to imagine it coming from Perelman's pen: the dissimilarity is immense. "It is a funny thing about the quality of the sunshine on a Sunday afternoon," Benchley begins.

On other days it is just sunshine and quite cheery in its middle-class way. But on Sunday afternoon it takes on a penetrating harshness which does nothing but show up the furniture. It doesn't make any difference where you are. You may be hanging around the Busy Bee lunch in Hong Kong, or polishing brass on a yacht in the North Sea; you may be out tramping across the estate of one of the vice presidents of a big trust company or teaching Indians to read in Arizona. The Sunday afternoon sunlight makes you dissatisfied with everything it hits. It has got to be stopped.[8]

Writing like this reminds us of something we might find in a castaway's bottle, for here we are listening to the very careful tones of a mind trapped on a desert island of sheer ennui. Benchley is writing an existential tract, and the world presented and implied in it is a world drained and bleached of meaning, a world not to be faced. Aside from the touches of gentle whimsey—"in its middle-class way," "It has got to be stopped"—the passage is a specimen existential tone-poem; Camus, Sartre, or the despairing Virginia Woolfe might have written it; and even though Benchley goes on to offer a couple of macabre comic antidotes to this reality-poisoning—he suggests that we set fire to the house "around 1:30" to create a little diverting excitement rather than endure that brutally meaningless slant of light—this does not really mitigate the very real dread that the passage expresses. V. S. Prichett, who has known many of our century's most talented comic writers, speaks of them as frequently "teetering on the edge of religious conversion or the hospital," and many times the sort of advanced neurotic who finds himself "hag-ridden by efficiency of mind."[9] The deepening psychological problems that assailed Benchley in his final years in Hollywood may indicate the sort of crisis an artist is vulnerable to when he feels he has exploited his gift to the point of its exhaustion and has nowhere left to turn; and Benchley seems to have recognized Perelman's superiority to him as a stylist, too, so he may have felt his way back to prose comedy was blocked, that his efforts there would be second best if not second rate. Speaking of Perelman, Benchley, a famously generous man, gave high and well-deserved praise—perhaps higher praise than he could afford to give. Perelman, he wrote, did to "our weak little efforts at 'crazy stuff' what Benny Goodman has done to middle-period jazz. He swung it. To use a swing phrase, he took it 'out of this world.' And there he remains, all by himself."[10] That Benchley's assessment remained true after Perelman had published "crazy stuff" for half a century is one measure of an impressive achievement.

The *New Yorker* School

Perelman's influence can also be discerned outside the world of the overtly comic writers. Professionals have always found Perelman's prose impressive and accorded it deep respect, and several writers would most likely not have written quite as they did if they had not been paying Perelman the sincerest form of flattery. For example, in some of his manic passages, we can find Thomas Pynchon, born in 1937, borrowing a tone from Perelman. About midway through *The*

Crying of Lot 49, Pynchon brings his heroine, Oedipa Maas (not a bad Perelmanesque name in itself), to a bush-league and very arty California theatrical. The play Oedipa sees at the Tank Theatre is a seventeenth-century revenger's tragedy called *The Courier's Tragedy* by one "Richard Wharfinger," and Pynchon describes its action for ten pages of his own book, obviously relishing the parodic possibilities it offers in a manner we might associate with one of Perelman's "Cloudland Revisited" pieces:

Attendance did not swell by the time the play started. But the costumes were gorgeous and the lighting imaginative, and though the words were all spoken in Transplanted Middle Western Stage British, Oedipa found herself after five minutes sucked utterly into the landscape of evil Richard Wharfinger had fashioned for his 17th-century audiences, so preapocalyptic, deathwishful, sensually fatigued, unprepared, a little poignantly, for that abyss of civil war that had been waiting, cold and deep, only a few years ahead of them.

Angelo, then, evil Duke of Squamuglia, has perhaps ten years before the play's opening murdered the good Duke of adjoining Faggio, by poisoning the feet on an image of Saint Narcissus, Bishop of Jerusalem, in the court chapel, which feet the Duke was in the habit of kissing every Sunday at Mass. This enables the evil illegitimate son, Pasquale, to take over as regent for his half-brother, Niccolo, the rightful heir and good guy of the play, till he comes of age. Pasquale of course has no intention of letting him live so long. Being in thick with the Duke of Squamuglia, Pasquale plots to do away with young Niccolo by suggesting a game of hide-and-seek and then finessing him into crawling inside of an enormous cannon, which a henchman is then to set off, hopefully blowing the child, as Pasquale recalls ruefully, later on in the third act,

> Out in a bloody rain to feed our fields
> Amid the Maenad roar of nitre's song
> And sulfur's cantus firmus.[11]

Pynchon's parody is obviously both literate and sophisticated, and it could only seem amusing to a reader with a humanities background and some knowledge of the American amateur stage. We recognize the accuracy of describing the speech affectations of these kind of actors as "Transplanted Middle Western Stage British," for the people who appear in provincial American theatricals *always* try to talk like Laurence Olivier or the Barrymores; and by including us in that sort of observation, Pynchon alerts us to his comic intention. Obviously, nothing here should be taken too solemnly. Further, Pynchon demonstrates the sort of expertise and command of detail that we have come to associate with Perelman. Anyone familiar with John Webster's blood-spattered dramas *The White Devil* or *The Duchess of Malfi*, or with Thomas Kyd's *The Spanish Tragedy*, will recognize that Pynchon's use of a poisoned icon as a murder weapon is hardly an exaggeration of seventeenth-century dramatic preposterousness, and Pynchon also assumes that we are sophisticated enough to recall that the Jacobean revenge drama reached its apogee only a few years before the English civil war began in 1641. Pasquale's iambic lines are a good imitation of Jacobean bombast, too, and they are also as accurate as Perelman's parodies in the use they make of specialized detail: thus, "Maenad roar"—the cry of an infuriated Bacchanate (such as one of those who tears Pentheus to pieces in Euripides' *The Bacche*)—is just the sort of reference from the classics a seventeenth-century play-wright would use to heighten his style for a tragic outcry, and the medieval Latin term "cantus firmus," plainsong, convinces us in passing that we are hearing an "authentic" period piece. But it is perhaps the playfulness of the rhetorical style and Pynchon's use of intentionally awkward or common turns of speech to bring the bombast down with a pratfall every couple of sentences that reminds us most insistently of Perelman: "the rightful heir *and good guy*"; "Pasquale of course has no intention of letting him *live so long*"; "being *in thick with the Duke*"; "*finessing him into* crawling inside"; and so on. Just as with Perelman's "Cloudland" parodies, this passage from *The Crying of Lot 49* exudes a wry sort of affection for the original it so expertly exaggerates. The tone of parody here, and the tone of the parodies in Perelman's canon, delights us vicariously with the fun it is so obviously having dressed up in those borrowed costumes. Perel-man's legacy to the future will no doubt show itself in the prose of highly self-conscious writers whose purposes will include the ac-knowledgment that they are writing—and having a damn good time of it, too.

William Zinsser's article on Perelman in the *New York Times Magazine* begins with a confession of his own "adolescent crush" on Perelman's prose, and he speaks of the "gravitational pull" of the famous Perelman style that "changed the shape of 20th-century humor."[12] Zinsser's claim is certainly no exaggeration, and it should not surprise us that it is in the work of some of his fellow *New Yorker* contributors that we can find the most vivid evidence of Perelman's "gravitational" influence.

Perelman's 1970 collection, *Baby, It's Cold Inside*, is dedicated to J. D. Salinger, and the professional admiration that the famous recluse must have felt for Perelman's work can be discerned on almost every page of the Glass family stories Salinger was writing during the middle and late 1950s. Here is Seymour Glass writing a word of advice to his younger brother Zooey, an actor:

I wish to God I had some idea what will happen to you as an actor. You're a born one, certainly. Even our [mother] Bessie knows that. And surely you and Franny are the only beauties in the family. But where will you act? Have you thought about it? The movies? If so, I'm scared stiff that if ever you gain any weight you'll be as victimized as the next young actor into contributing to the reliable Hollywood amalgam of prizefighter and mystic, gunman and underprivileged child, cowhand and Man's Conscience, and the rest. Will you be content with that standard box-office schmalz? Or will you dream of something a little more cosmic—zum Beispiel, playing Pierre or Andrey in a Technicolor production of *War and Peace* with stunning battlefield scenes, and all the nuances of characterization left out (on the ground that they're novelistic and unphotogenic), and Anna Magnani daringly cast as Natasha (just to keep the production classy and Honest), and gorgeous incidental music by Dmitri Popkin, and all the male leads intermittently rippling their jaw muscles to show they're under great emotional stress. . . .[13]

Martin Green points out that the prose in passages like this one calls attention to itself and exhibits "an outspoken desire to perform, to be entertaining and be entertained," and that this lack of self-restraint makes it "at first sight undignified."[14] But he goes on to note approvingly that although the irony of the passage obviously includes a satiric cutting edge, the self-conscious, hyperbolic, carnival tone of the piece causes the objects and proper nouns embedded in it to become "colorful, intricate, attractive." No writer could be more serious, even cosmic, than Salinger in his Glass family saga, for there he is determined to tell us a tale about nothing less than God's presence in an upper-middle-class apartment on Manhattan's East Seventies. But his work is anything but Dostoevskian, or properly "religious" in tone at all. It is playful, exuberant, endlessly self-conscious. It is always clowning. As Green insists so brilliantly, "the effect is not to communicate the disgust" Salinger's persona claims he is feeling: "What *we* feel, as we read, is a delighted recognition. Named in this way, these objects, our environment, becomes funny, vivid, glamorous, touching."[15] That I believe we find this effect almost everywhere in Perelman's work should by this point be axiomatic.

Vladimir Nabokov had made a coterie reputation for himself as a *New Yorker* writer long before he gave birth to the household words "Lolita" and "nymphet," and although Nabokov would be the last writer in our heritage to acknowledge any sort of influences on his own style, it would be hard to believe that the America that Humbert Humbert presents to us as he narrates *Lolita, or the Confession of a White Widowed Male* does not owe something to Perelman's genius. In fact, Nabokov never wrote in the same style, or even in a style very close to it, before or after *Lolita*, and it is important to notice that Humbert's perspective on mid-century teenage America is quite similar to that of Perelman's persona. Like Perelman's fictional alter egos, Humbert Humbert is far from morally immaculate (although not evil), and in both cases, the essential comic leverage is provided by the placement of an extraordinarily sophisticated, refined, and cosmopolitan intelligence in a milieu peopled with dulled nonentities and scheming vulgarians. And both writers' prose shows the same bumptious zest and self-conscious exuberance. Here Nabokov has his narrator describe a New England hotel called the Enchanted Hunters where Humbert has taken Lolita in order to seduce her:

There is nothing louder than an American hotel; and, mind you, this was supposed to be a quiet, cozy, old-fashioned, homey place—"gracious living" and all that stuff. The clatter of the elevator's gate—some twenty yards northeast of my head but as clearly perceived as if it were inside my left temple—alternated with the banging and booming of the machine's various evolutions and lasted well beyond midnight. Every now and then, immediately east of my left ear (always assuming I lay on my back, not daring to direct my viler side toward the nebulous haunch of my bed-mate) the corridor would brim with cheerful, resonant and inept exclamations ending in a volley of good-nights. When that stopped, a toilet immediately north of my cerebellum took over. It was a manly, energetic, deep-throated toilet, and it was used many times. Its gurgle and gush and long afterflow shook the wall behind me. Then someone in a southern direction was extravagantly sick, almost coughing out his life with his liquor, and his toilet descended like a veritable Niagara, immediately beyond our bathroom. And when finally all the waterfalls had stopped, and the enchanted hunters were sound asleep, the avenue under the window of my insomnia, to the west of my wake—a staid, eminently residential, dignified alley of huge trees—degenerated into the despicable haunt of gigantic trucks roaring through the wet and windy night. [16]

Like Perelman's, this is *poetic* prose—if we can recover that useful term from its connotations of fine writing. The experience is created with the aim of making us always *feel* the activity; and we are brought inside an imagination of real power as it perceives a particular place at a particular time. The lilt and precision of the words and images is admirable, the prose obviously polished and ordered with great care. And the distance between the expected and the actual creates an undertow of disillusion that allows us to realize we are in contact with psychological reality, always one attribute of first-rate comic prose.

Roger Angell, for about two decades a contributing editor for the *New Yorker*, may well be the writer of all writers whose style most obviously both owes and honors Perelman's achievement. Angell writes almost always about baseball, and just as with Perelman's travel pieces, a comic style in the service of journalism makes for a felicitous combination of play and photography, fun and realism. Here is Angell describing the first batter to face the New York Mets in their second season. Notice the smooth integration of dry baseball statistics and data with the metaphor of the volcano:

The first man to bat at the Polo Grounds in 1963 was a right-handed outfielder named Curt Flood, who plays for the St. Louis Cardinals. As he stepped up to the plate shortly after two o'clock on the afternoon of April 9, he was studied by me and the 25,848 other spectators at the park with an almost palpable apprehension. Flood represented the first hazard of the new season to the New York Mets, who had begun the previous season, the first of their existence, by losing the opening game to the Cardinals; had then tied a National League record by losing eight more games in succession; and had gone on to establish an all-time record by losing a hundred and twenty of the hundred and sixty games they played. During the endless, turbulent summer of 1962, Met fans and Met players developed a needlelike sensitivity to omens and portents, a superstitious belief in historical inevitability, and a fondness for disaster that were positively Sicilian, and here, on opening day, we gave Curt Flood the same apprehensive, defiant glare that a farmer on the slopes of Mount Etna might cast toward the smoke plume on the summit just before he began his spring lava-plowing. [17]

Angell's writing is as sophisticated and inventive as the average newspaper sports reportage is cliché-ridden and flat. He will characterize the long curls and luxurious facial hair of a young catcher as an "Oberammergau coiffure and beard," compare the chances of the Mets' relief pitchers to those of a "Balaclava cavalryman," or characterize Luis Tiant's famously deliberate pace on the pitcher's mound with a wonderful simile of Tiant pausing between pitches, "standing on the hill like a sunstruck archaeologist at Knossos." A fan hit with a foul ball hit by Rusty Staub looks "pained but ecstatic, like a man who has just received a personal message from Jove," and a young reporter addressing one of baseball's mossbacked old owners "shakes his head in the manner of a young lawyer who has undertaken to bring order out of his mother's checkbook." As far as many of us are concerned, Angell is the most gifted sports writer who has ever written in English-American, and there can be little doubt that his invention, his polish, and his witty, erudite references and allusive breadth owe a great deal to Perelman's example. It is a legacy he continues with reverence and great talent.

City Mice

Nothing can "explain" the individual artistic gift, but all artists are in part defined by the models available to them and the self-definitions of their eras. Few writers could be as unique as Perelman, as "sui generis to a fault"; but by this point we have accumulated some evidence of his place in a tradition of comic writing and the manner in which he has been the beneficiary of a certain heritage.

By the time that Perelman graduated from Brown in 1925, America had become an industrialized, sophisticated, and citified nation, and the city of cities for anyone of artistic inclinations was of course New York—specifically Greenwich Village, where Perelman immediately went to live after graduation. If, as has often been claimed, American comic achievement reached its apotheosis in the 1920s and 1930s, it was the natural culmination of a familiar social process. The country mice migrate to the city, or, to use Philip Rahv's formulation, the palefaces replace the redskins. At a certain point in the evolution of any nation, its Paris, London, or New York (or the metropolitan equivalent) becomes more than the nexus of material exchange and transport, it becomes an intellectual center and a center of style as well. This occurred in New York City just about the same time that Perelman came to it. Talented and well-educated people came to the Village, to Broadway, or to the numerous and varied journals and publishing concerns; this is not fresh news, or is the reason far to seek. It is always a safe generalization to say that talent will seek out its own opportunities and a congenial and rewarding environment. But it is perhaps less obvious to point out that history, which is always a matter of technology as well as of sociology, must cooperate. If Perelman, Benchley, Lardner, Alexander Woollcott, Dorothy Parker, Ogden Nash, Christopher Morley, Don Marquis, Heywood Broun, James Thurber, Cole Porter, George S. Kaufman, Moss Hart, Jerome Kern, George and Ira Gershwin, Richard Rodgers and Oscar Hammerstein, Nunnally Johnson, Marc Connelly, Harold Ross, E. B. White, Charles Brackett, and Frank Crowninshield (the founder of the glossy and sophisticated *Vanity Fair*) represent some of the dramatis personae of a glittering era in our cultural history, perhaps an era we will never see the likes of again, it should also be noted that the state of technology itself, circa 1925, helped allow this exciting New York Renaissance to happen. There was really no radio to speak of, television was a wild idea we would associate with the sort of people who hang around the waiting room at the patent office in a Charles Addams cartoon, and the movies would not learn to talk until 1927. An artist with words or music had his opportunity only on the page or the stage, and if Perelman is probably correct in assuming that a young talent with a comic bent starting out now would end up on a six-man joke-writing team in the televison mills, no such competition threatened the birth and growth of New York City prose and stage comedy in those days. This was crucial.

We have seen how the Algonquin group and the original editorial membership of the *New Yorker* deserted the East for Hollywood the moment the studios discovered that they needed some help mastering their difficult new obligation to speak. But mass art meant mass taste. Some writers like Faulkner, Aldous Huxley, John O'Hara, Evelyn Waugh, and Perelman had the integrity to see that the film money was not going to be worth the sacrifice. Given the choice between turning out claptrap at fancy prices or staying in the East and sticking to their last, most Eastern talents made the obvious and forgiveable choice and called a Beverly Hills real-estate agent. The movies would pay enormously; but then so would the writers who took their money. The lazy, silly, childish atmosphere of Hollywood eventually damaged them as artists, of course, but it is much too easy for those of us who have never been asked to join that golden harem to condemn a decision to succumb to the California sunshine and easy money. It is, after all, real sunshine and real money. Few have ever found writing comfortable and pleasant and easy, either, and Perelman's achievements have been paid for with nervous strain: "The effort of writing seems more arduous all the time,"[18] he went on record as saying, and we must feel a touch of shock and dismay when we overhear him saying that even his "Cloudland" pieces finally grew stale and repetitious for their creator: "Ultimately, I began to regard these matters as boring." Like most creative writers, he attested again and again to the fearsome difficulty of facing the blank page: "Any writer who tells you he's in a hurry to get to that desk is a faker, not a writer. . . ."[19] Perelman's choices were all the more impressive when we recall that he chose the stubborn, fussy, jealous, down-at-the-heel muse of pre-McLuhan print over the vapid but glamorous muse that presides like a beauty contest chaperone over the golden wasteland of movies and television. The fact that his integrity is our gain was his only real compensation.

The Future

Everyone agrees that American comic writing has taken a new turn in about the last fifteen years, but there has not been complete agreement as to why. As we have seen, Richard Freedman has noted that the "mainstream of recent humor" has been "cooler, more casual, less uptight" than the humor Perelman writes. It has also frequently been much crueler. While the mass media has enforced a castrating inoffensiveness on the comic material it presents—and Perelman and Groucho, both Jews, but both also gifted comics, bemoaned the fact that the media is so afraid of offending any and every minority that no ethnic humor of any sort is allowed to come over its immaculate airways[20]—comic writing for the minority audience has moved to change fear into farce, dread into laughter: it has become black humor or "neo-gothic." The contemporary writers we expect will turn out to be the most significant have all moved far beyond Perelman's safe little comic universe of Hollywood vulgarians and slow-witted customs clerks to make comedy out of war, sex, God, surgery, race, Mom, America and its presidents, and of course, death.

Joseph Heller's *Catch-22* appeared in 1961, and it is perhaps this antiwar novel that may serve as the most convenient dividing line between the old style of American comic writing and the writing that has come to at least partially supersede it, the new "sick" humor that has been called "black humor" or "neo-gothic." With *Catch-22*, a hilarious, brilliant, repetitious, preachy, overlong and unforgettable inversion of the war as fought by John Wayne, American comic writing turned to the darkness, the forbidden, the blasphemously negative, and the hilariously revolting. S. J. Perelman did not accompany it.

But it soon had company. In his 1963 novel *V.*, Thomas Pynchon included a five-page account of a surgical nose job on one Esther Harvitz, detailed right down to the last snip of scissors and snap of bone, a narrative interlude one critic confessed made him "so completely uncomfortable" that it required from him "an act of will to keep reading through it."[21] Robert Coover began a short story with the line, "In order to get started, he went to live alone on an island and shot himself."[22] Rudolph Wurlitzer's "Quake" takes us to a crumbling football stadium where the naked maniacs await the end of the world—the *real* end of the world. Philip Roth wrote an entire novel about a man who, in the best Kafka-fairy-tale tradition, found himself turned into a breast. Tom Stoppard took the two most inconsequential characters in *Hamlet* and wrote a hilarious existential tragedy starring the ciphers Rosencrantz and Guildenstern, and in order that no American minority group should go unoffended, Steve Katz began a story with the line, "Wonder Woman was a dike, but she was nice."[23] Ishmael Reed called his Western gunfighter town Yellow Back Radio and staged a race war with ghosts. The "roadside attraction" of Tom Robbins's first novel was the supposed body of Jesus Christ. In one of the eeriest innovations of all, E. L. Doctorow took historical personalities like Harry Houdini, Henry Ford, and J. P. Morgan and allowed them to speak and think as intimately as if they were the characters in a novel. Stanley Kubrick's film *Dr. Strangelove, or How I Started to Learn to Stop Worrying and Love the Bomb*, was the annunciation of a new sort of gallows hilarity, the punch line of which was a bang and not a whimper: the thermonuclear destruction of our planet. Times had indeed changed since *Dawn Ginsbergh's Revenge* was published in 1929. Humor had come to feed on the voluptuous absurdities of modern, postnuclear life, and the standard explanation for the shift in comic decorum from the playful and polite to the deadly and revolting, from safe humor to "sick" humor, was that a mirror, even a funhouse mirror, does not lie: "The simplest explanation for neo-gothic is that it reflects the present violence of American life—If nothing else, the neo-gothic phenomenon in fiction is an escalation brought about to attract audiences jaded by the routine of real horror on the evening news."[24] This comment by Joe David Bellamy is entirely representative of the general theoretical drift. The syllogism implied by it runs: fiction reflects reality; reality has come to be obscene, dangerous, and absurd; therefore fiction has come to be obscene, and absurd, and to at least reflect the cataclysmic dangers of the thermonuclear Sword of Damocles hanging above us. The syllogism is attractive because it is at once simple and all-

inclusive, and in some measure it may be as true as any such generalization about the state of an art can be. But at least one comment
relevent to our assessment of Perelman might be added to it.

Satire is a weapon, but parody is a toy. Whatever his private
feelings may be, as a professional writer Perelman is a one-man
F. A. O. Schwartz, a Santa's workshop of prose comedy. We know
that Perelman was disgusted and angry over the Vietnam stupidities,
but aside from the few stray comments he made to interviewers (and
his opinions were no angrier or more dismayed than those of the vast
majority of literate people), we find nothing about the war, satiric or
otherwise, in his professional prose. Watergate is not a target, nor
does Nixon furnish Perelman with comic possibilities. Nowhere does
he go after Joseph McCarthy, the Bay of Pigs, the CIA, or South
Africa. The drug culture and feminism lie untouched, not even the
subject of a single piece. These are remarkable omissions, made more
remarkable by comparison. In "The Schmeed Memoirs," Perelman's
disciple Woody Allen satirizes the good German, the little man who
only did his job and was neither expected to exert moral discrimina-
tion or choose against evil. Schmeed, Hitler's barber, assures us that
he was never "aware of the moral implications of what I was doing,"
and that "when I finally did find out what a monster Hitler was, it was
too late to do anything, as I had made a down payment on some
furniture. Once, toward the end of the war, I did contemplate
loosening the Führer's neck-napkin and allowing some tiny hairs to
get down his back, but at the last minute my nerve failed me."[25] Here
the humorist's irony hardly conceals the humanistic outrage that
drives it forward, but this is the sort of irony we never find in
Perelman. Style, not substance, was always his target—and by
"style" I want to indicate style in a relatively narrow sense: literary
style, verbal style, style in the visual arts, the debased styles of
Madison Avenue and television. Although he responded with great
irritation to interviewers who might tacitly recall him to the higher
purposes of satire—"I regard *my* comic writing as serious"—Perelman's work (if one must judge it as an instrument of correction) does
indeed lie outside the tradition of militant satire and wit in the service
of humanity. Perelman refused to engage the larger targets, and he
loathed the bandwagon of social virtue. He is on record as denouncing

as "dreary books" the "blizzard of ethnic novels about Negroes and Jews."[26]

"I don't believe in the importance of scale," Perelman once said with exasperation. "To me the muralist is no more valid than the miniature painter."[27] As I have tried to demonstrate, Perelman's masterful miniatures do show some traits that we can ascribe to an American-Jewish sensibility: the *shlemiel* is there, witnessing and suffering and trying to survive the outrage; the reverence for the great achievements of our literary culture is obviously there, even if couched in parodic form; and there is erudition for its own sake in a volume that would have impressed the most scholarly student of Joyce. Perelman realized the extent to which the Establishment is committed to self-glorifying propaganda, and his role as picador and deflater of pretension is traceable to his background as Jew and child of immigrants. One is always aware that he can *see* as much as anyone. He even knows that there exists out there something we have agreed to call "real life" and that there are indeed "real individuals, afflicted like the rest of us with bunions, flatulence, and presbyopia: folk who consult daily horoscopes, shlep their wetwash to the laundromat, fret about their sagging busts or their potency, and survive—God knows how—under the burden their parents have laid on them at the baptismal font."[28]

But the reader will look long and in vain for redeeming social value or Freudian significance in the objects of Perelman's wit: if that wit needs justification, it will have to be that of the comic catharsis as a therapeutic end in itself. Quixote's windmills seemed to the old mad knight to be the powers of darkness; if Perelman's targets were evil, it was evil reduced to the size of a pinwheel. To try to justify his charm by appeal to its social importance is to miss the point. Perelman's devotion to style as a value in and of itself must finally be regarded as the source of his enduring appeal—early and late, Perelman the miniaturist knew what he wanted to do, and he did it more than well, he did it once and for all. Of course he seems to us at the moment more than a little out of fashion and dated; tastes inevitably change.

In 1970 Eudora Welty said in regard to Perelman that "folly is perennial, but something happened to parody. Life has caught up with it. . . . Parody is among the early casualties of this [capture],

for it comes to be no longer recognizable apart from its subject."[29]
Perhaps Perelman seems a bit dated because the shared aesthetic
standards necessary for parody have vanished; or perhaps we see the
modern world, blackened as it is with the chimney-ashes of Auschwitz and with its important energies in the hands of the corporations
and the military, as so monstrously wrong that we cannot find much
delight in a toy parody that makes such gentle but ineffectual fun out
of its errors of speech, manner, and the fatuity of its popular arts.
Those who find Perelman old-fashioned might also see that his
distinctive gift for creating a unique style and comic world of his own
have allowed us to take it too much for granted, so that, as William
Zinsser says, "inevitably, some of the surprise is gone"[30] after all these
years. But this is to speak of Perelman as an artist widely published for
fifty years, as read by Americans in the midst of a long, fatiguing
crisis in national morale. Like all artists of great and original gifts,
Perelman will weather the future, and Alan Brien may well be right
when he predicts that "School boys and girls yet unborn, studying the
origins of the twenty-first century's dominant tongue, Anglo-Amer-
ican, may find in Perelman its first assured master, fusing the heritage
of Twain and Hazlitt."[31] We all know the truth in Auden's famous
observation tht Time loves words and forgives all those who live by
them, and we can be sure that Perelman's ingenious and superbly
crafted work will be cherished as one of the most unique and durable
achievements of our literary era.

Notes and References

Chapter One

1. Alan Brien, "S. J. Perelman: the Man in the Ironic Mask," *Quest/78* November, 1978, p. 93.

2. Jane Howard, "Close-up: S. J. Perelman—the Cranky Humorist," *Life*, February 9, 1962, p. 93.

3. *The Most of S. J. Perelman* (New York, 1958): hereafter cited in the text as *M*.

4. *Chicken Inspector No. 23* (New York, 1966), p. 239.

5. *Life*, February 9, 1962, p. 86.

6. William Zinsser, "The Perelman of Great Price Is 65," *New York Times Magazine*, January 26, 1965, p. 76.

7. Charles Moritz and H. W. Wilson, eds., *Current Biography Yearbook 1971* (New York, 1972), p. 322.

8. Eudora Welty, review of *Baby, It's Cold Inside, New York Times Book Review*, August 30, 1970, p. 1.

9. *Baby, It's Cold Inside* (New York, 1970), p. 40.

10. Ibid., p. 79.

11. *The Rising Gorge* (New York, 1961), p. 245.

12. Zinsser, p. 72.

13. John Hollander, ed., *American Short Stories Since 1945* (New York: Harper & Row, 1968), p. xiii.

14. Brien, p. 74.

15. Zinsser, p. 26.

16. Jay Martin, *Nathanael West: the Art of His Life* (New York, 1970), p.74.

17. Moritz and Wilson, p. 320.

18. Martin, p. 68.

19. Ibid., p. 67.

20. Ibid., p. 57.

21. Ibid., p. 74.

22. *The Road to Miltown* (New York, 1957), p. 210.

23. *Chicken Inspector No. 23*, p. 251.

24. Ibid., p. 252.

25. Ibid., p. 253.

26. *Baby, It's Cold Inside*, pp. 171–72.

27. *Chicken Inspector No. 23*, p. 253.

28. *Baby, It's Cold Inside*, p. 171.

29. Roy Newquist, *Conversations* (New York, 1967), p. 276.

30. "The Winsome Foursome: How to Go Batty with the Marx Brothers when Writing a Film Called *Monkey Business*," *Show*, November, 1961, p. 34.

31. Martin, p. 109.

32. Ibid., p. 118.

33. *Chicken Inspector No. 23*, p. 254.

34. Joe Adamson, *Groucho, Harpo, Chico and Sometimes Zeppo: a Celebration of the Marx Brothers* (New York: Simon and Schuster, 1973), p. 171.

35. Ibid., p. 117.

36. *Show*, November, 1961, p. 36.

37. Ibid., p. 37.

38. Ibid.

39. Adamson, p. 135.

40. *Show*, November, 1961, p. 38.

41. Adamson, pp. 135, 136, 144, 143, 139, 141.

42. Quoted in Adamson, p. 144. The film script is available in book form: *The Four Marx Brother in "Monkey Business" and "Duck Soup"* (New York, 1972).

43. *Take One*, September–October, 1970, p. 37.

44. *Guardian*, November 30, 1970, p. 16.

45. Arthur Marx, *Son of Groucho* (New York: David McKay, 1972), p. 105.

46. "The Hollywood Metaphor: the Marx Brothers, S. J. Perelman, and Nathanael West," *Southern Review* 12 (Summer, 1976): 660–65.

47. Zinsser, p. 26.

48. Adamson, p. 185.

49. Allen Eyles, *The Marx Brothers: Their World of Comedy* (New York: A. S. Barnes, 1966), p. 62.

50. Moritz and Wilson, p. 320.

51. Newquist, p. 279.

52. William Cole and George Plimpton, *Writers at Work: the Paris Review Interviews: Second Series* (New York, 1963), p. 252.

53. Pauline Kael, *The Citizen Kane Book: Raising Kane* (Boston: Little, Brown, 1971), p. 11.

54. Cole and Plimpton, p. 251.

55. F. Scott Fitzgerald, *The Last Tycoon* (New York: Scribner's, 1970), pp. 159–60.

56. Michael Davie, ed., *The Diaries of Evelyn Waugh* (London: Weidenfeld and Nicolson, 1976), p. 788.

57. "Hail to the Chief, at Two-Thirds Off," *Chicken Inspector No. 23.*

58. Newquist, p. 280.

59. *New York Times Theater Reviews* (New York: Arno Press, 1971) for December 6, 1933.

60. *New York Times Film Reviews* (New York: Arno Press, 1970), p. 1082.

61. Martin, p. 310.

62. Zinsser, p. 26.

63. Reviewed by Bosley Crowther for the *Times* (February 9, 1939); reprinted in *The New York Times Film Reviews*, p. 1576.

64. *Newsweek*, January 30, 1939, p. 24.

65. *New York Times Film Reviews*, p. 1746.

66. *The New York Times*, April 11, 1941, p. 25.

67. *New York Times Film Reviews*, p. 1861.

68. Fitzgerald, p. 125.

69. The Triangle Shirtwaist Factory was a Manhattan garment-center sweatshop which burned up in 1911, causing 142 deaths. The grisly in-joke was thus Eastern, urban, and Jewish, the background of so many of Hollywood's imported writers.

70. Martin, p. 345.

71. Ibid., p. 310.

72. Perelman's 1959 television comedy *Malice in Wonderland* features a psychiatrist (played by Keenan Wynn) in Hollywood.

73. *Baby, It's Cold Inside*, p. 133.

74. Ibid., p. 134.

75. Sheila Graham, *The Garden of Allah* (New York: Crown, 1970), p. 72.

76. *The Road to Miltown*, p. 242.

77. *Eastward Ha!* (New York, 1977), p. 117.

78. *Show*, November, 1961, p. 32.

79. *New York Times*, November 30, 1930, p. 9.

80. *Saturday Review of Literature*, July 12, 1930, p. 1195.

81. Reviewed by John Hutchens for the *Times*, June 2, 1931; reprinted in *The New York Times Theater Reviews* for that date.

82. *New York Times*, June 2, 1931.

83. *New York Times*, December 8, 1932, p. 24.

84. *The Rising Gorge*, p. 178.
85. *New Republic*, September 1, 1937, p. 108.
86. *Saturday Review of Literature*, July 31, 1937, p. 21.

Chapter Two

1. *Time*, October 29, 1956, p. 72.
2. Newquist, p. 280.
3. *Vinegar Puss* (New York, 1975), p. 35.
4. *Time*, October 29, 1956, p. 72.
5. *Vinegar Puss*, p. 35.
6. *Holiday*, October, 1956, p. 112.
7. *Time*, October 29, 1956, p. 72.
8. *New Yorker*, October 27, 1956, p. 158.
9. *Newsweek*, November 5, 1956, p. 115.
10. Maralyn Lois Polak, "S. J. Perelman: He's America's Lampoonist Laureate," in *Authors in the News* (Detroit, 1976), p. 219.
11. Ibid., p. 219.
12. *Vinegar Puss*, p. 44.
13. Polak, p. 219.
14. *Vinegar Puss*, p. 46.
15. Ibid., pp. 50, 51, 58.
16. Newquist, p. 285.
17. This was Mary Martin's first starring role. She had created a sensation in Cole Porter's *Leave It To Me* (1938) with a sexy rendering of "My Heart Belongs to Daddy."
18. *The Groucho Letters* (New York, 1967), p. 190.
19. Beckerman and Siegman, *On Stage: Theatre Reviews from the New York Times* (New York, 1971), p. 248.
20. *New York Theater Critics' Reviews* (New York: Critics' Theatre Reviews, Inc., 1943), pp. 264–66.
21. *New York Times Film Reviews*, p. 2286.
22. Marilyn Stasio, *Broadway's Beautiful Losers* (New York, 1972), p. 158.
23. Ibid., p. 176
24. John Lahr, *Up Against the Fourth Wall* (New York, 1970), p. 80.
25. Richard Gilman, *Common and Uncommon Masks* (New York, 1970), p. 213.
26. Ibid., p. 213.
27. *New York Times*, January 5, 1963, sec. 5, p. 1.
28. *New York Theater Critics' Reviews*, p. 162.

29. Stasio, p. 164.

30. Ibid., p. 165.

31. Ibid., p. 162.

32. Ibid., p. 175.

33. "Funny Man," *New Yorker*, January 26, 1963, p. 25.

34. Stasio, p. 168.

35. Ibid., p. 162.

36. *Chicken Inspector No. 23*, p. 56.

37. Stasio, p. 166.

38. *New York Times Book Review*, July 21, 1963, p. 22.

39. Ward, p. 660.

40. Lahr, p. 163.

41. Stasio, p. 159.

42. Vladimir Nabokov, *Invitation to a Beheading* (New York: Capricorn Books, 1965), p. 7.

43. *The Rising Gorge,* p. 177.

44. Ibid., p. 67.

45. Prose pieces that were recycled into *The Beauty Part* include "The Hand That Cradles the Rock," "De Gustibus Ain't What Dey Used to Be" (both included in *The Most of S. J. Perelman*), and "Portrait of the Artist as a Young Mime" and "Oh, I Am a Cook and a Houseboy Bland" (both in *The Rising Gorge*).

46. Stasio, p. 167.

47. Ibid., p. 166.

48. "Talk with the Author," *Newsweek*, January 7, 1963, p. 59.

49. Stasio, p. 169.

Chapter Three

1. Newquist, p. 286.

2. Ibid., p. 278.

3. Originally published September 18, 1970; reprinted in *The New York Times Biographical Edition for 1970*, p. 2313.

4. *Life*, February 9, 1962, p. 93.

5. Shenker, p. 364.

6. George Orwell, *A Collection of Essays* (New York: Harcourt, Brace, Jovanovich, 1954), p. 258.

7. Polak, p. 219.

8. Ibid., p. 219.

9. Brien, p. 85.

10. Ibid., p. 77.

11. Polak, p. 220

12. Brien, p. 78.

13. Felicia Lamport, "The Perils of Perelman," *New Republic*, March 29, 1975, p. 23.

14. Zinsser, p. 76.

15. In Robert Kimball, ed., *Cole* (New York: Holt, Rinehart & Winston, 1971), p. xix.

16. George Eells, *The Life That Late He Led* (New York: G. P. Putnam's, 1967), p. 306.

17. Eells, p. 307.

18. *New York Times*, February 22, 1958, p. 33.

19. Reprinted in Moritz and Wilson, p. 321.

20. *Chicken Inspector No. 23*, p. 242.

21. *Vinegar Puss*, p. 110.

22. Zinsser, p. 26.

23. Polak, p. 220.

24. "Cloudland Remembered: S. J. Perelman Presents the New York Film Critics' Screenplay Award to *Annie Hall*," *Film Comment*, March—April, 1978, p. 25.

25. *The Rising Gorge*, p. 155.

26. Ibid., p. 157.

27. Ibid., p. 160.

28. Reprinted in *Vinegar Puss*.

29. *Vinegar Puss*, p. 187.

30. Ibid., p. 187.

31. Ibid., p. 188.

32. Ibid., p. 189.

33. Reprinted in Ibid.

34. Ibid., p. 82.

35. Ibid., p. 83.

36. Philip Hamburger, "Unforgettable S. J. Perelman," *Reader's Digest*, March, 1980, pp. 99—103.

37. Hope Hale Davis, "The Sad Side of Perelman," *The New Leader*, July 27, 1981, p. 17.

Chapter Four

1. Polak, p. 219—20.

2. Reprinted in *Biography News*, January—February, 1975, p. 169.

3. Moritz and Wilson, p. 319.

4. Cole and Plimpton, pp. 254, 248.

5. Zinsser, p. 76.

6. Ibid.

7. John Lahr, *Prick Up Your Ears* (New York: Knopf, 1978), p. xi.

8. Newquist, p. 284.

9. Arthur Koestler, *The Act of Creation* (New York: Macmillan, 1964), p. 52.

10. T. S. Eliot, "Tradition and the Individual Talent," in *The Sacred Wood* (London: Methuen, 1920), p. 53.

11. Louis Hasley, "The Kangaroo Mind of S. J. Perelman," *South Atlantic Quarterly* 72 (Winter, 1973): 115−21.

12. Richard Freedman, *Book World*, September, 1970, p. 9.

13. Edith Oliver, "Return of a Winner," *New Yorker*, November 11, 1974, p. 106.

14. Dick Brukenfield, "A Gadfly Is a Bad Fly," *Village Voice*, November 7, 1974, p. 83.

15. Zinsser, p. 76.

16. Irving Goffman, "Self-Presentation," in *Satire*, ed. Ronald Paulson (Englewood Cliffs, N.J.: Prentice-Hall, 1971), p. 27.

17. Quoted in Irving Howe, *World of Our Fathers* (New York: Simon and Schuster, 1976), p. 14.

18. Robert Alter, "Jewish Humor and the Domestication of Myth" in *Veins of Humor*, ed. Harry Levin (Cambridge, Mass., 1972), p. 257.

19. Hasley, p. 117.

20. Mark Shechner, "Jewish Writers," in *The Harvard Guide to Contemporary American Writing*, ed. Daniel Hoffman (Cambridge, Mass.: Harvard University Press, 1979), p. 220.

21. Mark Harris, *Saul Bellow, Drumlin Woodchuck* (Athens: University of Georgia Press, 1980), p. 12.

22. Saul Bellow, *Mr. Sammler's Planet* (New York: Viking Press, 1970), p. 71.

23. J. D. Salinger, *Nine Stories* (Boston: Little, Brown, 1953), p. 104.

24. Robert Alter, *Defenses of the Imagination* (Berkeley: University of California Press, 1978), pp. 163−64.

25. Howe, p. 570.

26. Ibid., p. 587.

27. Ibid., p. 483.

28. Ibid., p. 460.

29. Scott Meredith, *George S. Kaufman* (Garden City, N.Y.: Doubleday, 1974), p. 432.

30. Ibid., p. 453.

31. Ward, p. 660.

32. Albert Goldman, "The Comedy of Lenny Bruce," *Commentary*, October, 1963, p. 314.

33. Leo Rosten, *The Joys of Yiddish* (New York: McGraw-Hill, 1968), p. 169.

34. Ruth R. Wisse, *The Schlemiel as Modern Hero* (Chicago: University of Chicago Press, 1971), p. 14.

35. Ibid., p. 16.

36. Howe, p. 571.

37. Wisse, p. 6.

38. Ibid., p. 3.

39. Woody Allen, *Without Feathers* (New York: Random House, 1963), p. 5.

40. Peter Gay, *Freud, Jews, and Other Germans* (New York: Oxford University Press, 1978), p. 154.

41. Sanford Pinsker, "Jumping on Hollywood's Bones, or How S. J. Perelman and Woody Allen Found It at the Movies," *Midwest Quarterly*, Spring, 1980, p. 379.

42. Philip Roth, *Reading Myself and Others* (New York: Farrar, Straus and Giroux, 1975), p. 138.

43. Howe, pp. 566–67.

44. *Biography News*, January/February, 1975, p. 170.

Chapter Five

1. Newquist, p. 281.

2. *Eastward Ha!*, p. 14.

3. *New York Times*, August 21, 1948, p. 5.

4. Cole and Plimpton, p. 246.

5. "The Wild Blue Yonder," *Holiday*, December, 1949, p. 76.

6. "Our Author's Portable Martriarchy Fearlessly Braves the Miniscule Perils of Bali and Bangkok," *Holiday*, August, 1950, p. 61.

7. Lee Rogow, *Saturday Review of Literature*, December 16, 1950, p. 17.

8. Richardson Wright, *New York Herald Tribune Weekly Book Review*, August 10, 1947, p. 2.

9. Richard Maloney, *New York Times*, August 24, 1947, p. 6.

10. Brien, p. 75.
11. "How Ruritanian Can You Get," *New Yorker*, January 22, 1949, p. 23.
12. Ibid.
13. *The Road to Miltown* (New York, 1957), p. 7.
14. Paul Theroux, "No Buff for the Briefalo," *The New York Times Book Review*, October 2, 1977, p. 9.
15. J. D. Salinger, *The Catcher in the Rye* (Boston: Little, Brown, 1951), pp. 169–70.
16. Cole and Plimpton, p. 248.
17. Paul Theroux, "Marxist," *New Statesman*, April 9, 1976, p. 476.
18. *Chicken Inspector No. 23*, p. 57.
19. *Eastward Ha!*, p. 38.
20. M. H. Abrams, *A Glossary of Literary Terms* (New York: Rinehart, 1971), p. 179.
21. George Orwell, *A Collection of Essays* (New York: Harcourt, Brace & Jovanovich, 1954), p. 100.
22. Vladimir Nabokov, *Bend Sinister* (New York: Time-Life Books, 1964), p. xvii.
23. *Vinegar Puss,* p. 169.

Chapter Six

1. Newquist, p. 286
2. George Ade, *Fables in Slang* (New York: Stone, 1900), p. 38.
3. William Zinsser, *On Writing Well* (New York: Harper & Row, 1980), p. 168.
4. Quoted in Bier, p. 209.
5. Cole and Plimpton, p. 247.
6. Walter Blair and Hamlin Hill, *America's Humor: from Poor Richard to Doonesbury* (New York, 1978), p. 433.
7. Ibid., p. 435.
8. Robert Benchley, *The Benchley Roundup* (New York: Harper & Row, 1954), p. 157.
9. V. S. Pritchett, "The Con-man's Shadow," *New Statesman*, November 24, 1967, p. 719.
10. Blair and Hill, p. 433.
11. Thomas Pynchon, *The Crying of Lot 49* (Philadelphia: Lippincott, 1966), pp. 44–45.
12. Zinsser, p. 25.

13. J. D. Salinger, *Franny and Zooey* (Boston: Little, Brown, 1961), pp. 60−61.

14. Martin Green, *Re-Appraisals* (New York: Norton, 1965), p. 212.

15. Ibid., p. 215.

16. Alfred Appel, Jr., ed., *The Annotated Lolita* (New York: McGraw-Hill, 1970), pp. 131−32.

17. Roger Angell, *The Summer Game* (New York: Viking, 1972), p. 83.

18. Cole and Plimpton, p. 245.

19. Shenker, p. 366.

20. Kenneth Tynan, *Tynan Right and Left* (New York: Atheneum, 1967), p. 327.

21. George Levin, "Risking the Moment," in *Mindful Pleasures: Essays on Thomas Pynchon*, ed. George Levin and David Leverenz (Boston: Little, Brown, 1976), p. 119.

22. Quoted in Tom Wolfe, ed., *The New Journalism* (New York: Harper & Row, 1973), p. 29.

23. Steve Katz, "Mythology: Wonder Woman," in *Innovative Fiction*, ed. Jerome Klinkowitz (New York: Dell, 1972), p. 158.

24. Joe David Bellamy, *Superfiction* (New York: Random House, 1975), p. 10.

25. Woody Allen, "The Schmeed Memoirs," in *Getting Even* (New York: Random House, 1971), p. 38.

26. Newquist, p. 279.

27. Cole and Plimpton, p. 255.

28. Quoted from his preface to John Train, ed., *Remarkable Names of Real People* (New York: C. N. Potter, 1977), p. 8.

29. Eudora Welty, *New York Times Book Review*, August 30, 1970, p. 1.

30. Zinsser, p. 76.

31. Brien, p. 73.

Selected Bibliography

PRIMARY SOURCES

1. Collections
The Best of S. J. Perelman. New York: Modern Library, 1947.
The Most of S. J. Perelman. New York: Simon and Schuster, 1958.

2. Books, Plays, and Films
Acres and Pains. New York: Reynal, 1947.
Ambush. Paramount, 1939. Screenplay by S. J. and Laura Perelman, based
    on a story by Robert Day.
Around the World in Eighty Days. United Artists, 1956. Screenplay by Perel-
    man, James Poe, and John Farrow, based on the novel by Jules Verne.
Baby, It's Cold Inside. New York: Simon and Schuster, 1970.
The Beauty Part. New York: Simon and Schuster, 1961.
Chicken Inspector No. 23. New York: Simon and Schuster, 1966.
Crazy Like a Fox. New York: Random House, 1944.
Dawn Ginsbergh's Revenge. New York: Liveright, 1929.
The Dream Department. New York: Random House, 1943.
Eastward Ha! New York: Simon and Schuster, 1977.
Florida Special. Paramount, 1936. Screenplay by David Boehm, Marguerite
    Roberts, and S. J. and Laura Perelman, based on a story by Clarence
    B. Kelland.
The Four Marx Brothers in "Monkey Business" and "Duck Soup." New York:
    Simon and Schuster, 1972.
The Golden Fleecing. MGM, 1940. Screenplay by Marion Parsonnet, and
    S. J. and Laura Perelman, from a story by Lynn Root and Frank Fenton.
Horse Feathers. Paramount, 1932. Screenplay by Harry Ruby, Bert Kalmar,
    and Perelman.
The Ill-Tempered Clavicord. New York: Simon and Schuster, 1952.
Keep It Crisp. New York: Random House, 1946.
Larceny, Inc. Warner Brothers, 1942. Screenplay by Everett Freeman and
    Edwin Gilbert, from the play *The Night Before Christmas*, by S. J.
    and Laura Perelman.

The Last Laugh. New York: Simon and Schuster, 1981.

Listen to the Mocking Bird. New York: Simon and Schuster, 1949.

Look Who's Talking. New York: Random House, 1949.

Monkey Business. Paramount Publix, 1931. Screenplay by Will Johnstone and Perelman.

One Touch of Venus. Boston: Little, Brown, 1944.

One Touch of Venus. Universal-International, 1948. Screenplay by Harry Kurnitz and Frank Tashlin, based on a stage musical by Ogden Nash and Perelman.

Parlor, Bedlam, and Bath. With Quentin Reynolds, Jr. New York: Liveright, 1930.

Perelman's Home Companion. New York: Simon and Schuster, 1955.

The Rising Gorge. New York: Simon and Schuster, 1961.

The Road to Miltown. New York: Simon and Schuster, 1957.

The Swiss Family Perelman. New York: Simon and Schuster, 1950.

Vinegar Puss. New York: Simon and Schuster, 1975.

Westward Ha! or Around the World in Eighty Clichés. New York: Simon and Schuster, 1948.

For the best available, though incomplete, list of the separate publications of Perelman's "casuals" see Steven H. Gale, "S. J. Perelman: Twenty Years of American Humor," *Bulletin of Bibliography* 29 (January—March, 1972): 10—12, an invaluable listing of the books and 171 short essays between 1940 and 1960.

SECONDARY SOURCES

Alter, Robert. "Jewish Humor and the Domestication of Myth." In *Veins of Humor*, edited by Harry Levin. Cambridge: Harvard University Press, 1972, pp. 255—79. Intelligent and persuasive.

"'Appalled' Perelman Going Eastward Ha!" *New York Times Biographical Edition.* New York: New York Times Co., 1970. (Reprint of an article that appeared September 18, 1970), p. 2313. Perelman's acid commentary on New York City as he left it for London.

Beckerman, Bernard, and **Siegman, Howard,** eds. *On Stage: Selected Theatre Reviews from the New York Times 1920—1970.* New York: Quadrangle, 1973. Review of *One Touch of Venus* and *The Beauty Part.*

Bier, Jesse. *The Rise and Fall of American Humor.* New York: Holt, Rinehart and Winston, 1968. Admirable research, ambitious (and highly suspect) theoretical approach; notes that Perelman's devotion to style has preserved the freshness of his work for more than a generation.

Blair, Walter. *Horse Sense in American Humor, from Benjamin Franklin to Odgen Nash.* Chicago: University of Chicago, 1942. An attempt to place Perelman in the context of the American humorous tradition.

———, and Hill, Hamlin. "Benchley and Perelman." In *America's Humor: from Poor Richard to Doonesbury.* New York: Oxford University Press, 1978, pp. 427–36. First-rate analysis of Perelman's use of fantasy in contrast to Benchley and others. The book itself is perhaps the best study to date on the American comic tradition.

Brickman, Marshall. "Inimitable Perelman." *Saturday Review of Literature,* July, 1981, pp. 68, 71. Posthumous tribute by Woody Allen's film collaborator: "He was the maestro, nonpareil, incomparable, beyond interpretation."

Brien, Alan. "S. J. Perelman: the Man in the Ironic Mask." *Quest/78,* November, 1978, pp. 71-74, 76. Personal and essential.

Brukenfield, Dick. "A Gadfly is a Bad Fly." *The Village Voice,* November 7, 1974. Bad-tempered dissent on the revival of *The Beauty Part.*

"Cloudland Remembered: S. J. Perelman presents the New York Film Critics' Screenplay Award to *Annie Hall.*" *Film Comment,* March–April, 1978, p. 25. Perelman reminisces on his days at MGM and praises Woody Allen.

Cole, William, and Plimpton, George. *Writers at Work: the Paris Review Interviews: Second series.* New York: Viking, 1963, pp. 241–56. Funny and fascinating glimpses of the artist in the toils of creative agony.

Esslin, Martin. *The Theatre of the Absurd.* New York: Doubleday, 1961. Perelman's contributions to the Marx Brothers' films in turn "directly influenced" Ionesco, Genet, Beckett, and Albee.

"Funny Man." *New Yorker,* January 26, 1963, pp. 25–27. Bert Lahr on the best comedy material he had ever had, *The Beauty Part.*

Gilman, Richard. *Common and Uncommon Masks: Writings on the Theatre 1961-1970.* New York: Random House, 1971. Contains an unsympathetic but fair review-essay of *The Beauty Part,* praising Bert Lahr but finding Perelman's play "too verbal."

Hamburger, Philip. "Unforgettable S. J. Perelman." *Reader's Digest,* March, 1980, pp. 99–103. Elegiac reminiscence.

Hasley, Louis. "The Kangaroo Mind of S. J. Perelman." *South Atlantic*

Quarterly 72 (Winter, 1973); 115−21. Good article stressing Perelman's underlying reasonableness.

Howard, Jane. "Close-up: S. J. Perelman−the Cranky Humorist." *Life*,
February 9, 1962, pp. 85−93. Photos and interview on the occasion
of *The Beauty Part*.

Kael, Pauline. *The Citizen Kane Book*. Boston: Little, Brown, 1971. Fascinating glimpses of Hollywood intellectuals in backdrop of portrait
of Herman J. Mankiewicz, producer of the Marx brothers comedies.

"Keats to the Ducks." *Newsweek*, July 15, 1963, p. 77. On the television
special *Elizabeth Taylor's London*, for which Perelman wrote the con-
tinuity.

Kramer, Dale. *Ross and the New Yorker*. New York: Doubleday, 1952.
Genesis of the great magazine; notes Perelman's meticulous and ex-
acting rewrites.

Kunitz, Stanley J., and Haycraft, Howard, eds. *Twentieth Century Authors:
a Biographical Dictionary of Modern Literature*. First supplement. New
York: H. W. Wilson, pp. 771−72. Bits of reviews and biography in
extreme summary.

Lahr, John. *Up Against the Fourth Wall*. New York: Grove, 1970. Good
analysis of strengths and deficiencies of *The Beauty Part* by the son
of its star.

Leacock, Stephen. *Humor and Humanity: an Introduction to the Study of
Humor*. New York: Henry Holt, 1938. Leacock was one of the literary
antecedents Perelman was proud to claim, but this book tries to
prove that "humor and human kindliness are one," a statement with
which Perelman would never agree.

Leyda, Jay, ed. *Voices of Film Experience*. New York: Macmillan, 1977.
Scraps of insight and reminiscence from the dream factory, 1894 to
present.

Martin, Jay. *Nathanael West: the Art of His Life*. New York: Farrar, Straus
and Giroux, 1970. The definitive biography of Perelman's brother-in-
law includes a good deal of material on Perelman and Laura.

Marx, Groucho. *The Groucho Letters*. New York: Simon and Schuster,
1967. Letters to and from the great comic include several from Perelman.

Moritz, Charles, ed. *Current Biography Yearbook*. New York: H. W.
Wilson, 1971, pp. 319−22. Interviews, biographical items, and bits
of reviews in potpourri.

Newquist, Roy. *Conversations*. New York: Rand McNally, 1967, pp.
275−86. Interesting and detailed interview in which Perelman stresses

his sense of tradition, his literary admirations (Twain, Ade, Lardner, Benchley, et al.), and reaffirms his "sole ambition" to write as well as he can in the form of the short comic essay.

Pinsker, Sanford. "Jumping on Hollywood's Bones, or How S. J. Perelman and Woody Allen Found It at the Movies." *Midwest Quarterly*, vol. xxi, no. 3 (Spring, 1980); 371–83. Interesting affinities.

Polak, Maralyn Lois. "S. J. Perelman: He's America's Lampoonist Laureate." *Philadelphia Enquirer*, March 30, 1975. Reprinted in *Authors in the News*, vol. 2 (Detroit: Gale, 1976), p. 219. Chatty interview.

Porter, Amy. "Garden of Allah, I Love You." *Collier's*, November 22, 1947, pp. 18–19, 102, 105. Humdrum piece on the haunt of Hollywood intellectuals and literati.

Seldes, Gilbert. *The Seven Lively Arts*. Rev. ed. New York: Harper, 1924. Popular culture of the 1920s attractively recalled.

Shenker, Israel. *Words and Their Masters*. New York: Doubleday, 1974, pp. 18–20, 202–4, 364–68. Three interviews, before and after Perelman's flight to England.

Stasio, Marilyn. *Broadway's Beautiful Losers*. New York: Delacorte Press, 1972. Excellent discussions of five plays that failed undeservedly; Stasio's indictment of Broadway as a poorly managed industry includes interesting insights into the realities of theatrical production.

"Talk with the Author." *Newsweek*, January 7, 1963, pp. 58–59. All about *The Beauty Part*.

Theroux, Paul. "Marxist." *New Statesman* 96 (April 9, 1976); 476. Excellent short analysis of Perelman's affinity for Joyce by a brilliant contemporary writer.

———. "No Buff for the Briefalo." *New York Times Book Review*, October 2, 1977, p. 9. Review of *Eastward Ha!* by an eloquent enthusiast.

Ward, J. A. "The Hollywood Metaphor: the Marx Brothers, S. J. Perelman and Nathanael West." *Southern Review* 12 (Summer, 1976): 659–72. Interesting analysis of Perelman's use of Hollywood fantasy.

Welty, Eudora. *"Baby, It's Cold Inside."* *New York Times Book Review*, August 30, 1970, pp. 1, 25. Excellent analysis connecting Perelman's concerns to "sadness" and "outrage."

Wolfe, Tom. "The Exploits of El Sid." *The New York Times Book Review*, July 19, 1981, pp. 1, 16. Acknowledges Perelman "as one of American literature's perfect but limited talents" but complains that he too seldom made "a warrior's heedless charge into realism."

Yates, Norris W. "The Sane Psychoses of S. J. Perelman." *The American*

Humorist: Conscience of the Twentieth Century. Ames: Iowa State University, 1964, pp. 331—50. Doctrinaire effort to show that Perelman's comic efforts are good medicine.

Zinsser, William. "The Perelman of Great Price is 65." *New York Times Magazine*, January 26, 1969, pp. 25—26, 72—74, 76. Invaluable article on career.

Index